Living the Eucharist

Affirming Catholicism and the Liturgy

Edited by
STEPHEN CONWAY

Introduced by
DAVID STANCLIFFE

DARTON·LONGMAN + TODD

First published in 2001 by
Darton, Longman and Todd Ltd
1 Spencer Court
140–142 Wandsworth High Street
London SW18 4JJ

Reprinted 2002

ISBN 0-232-52421-1

Phototypeset by Intype London Ltd

Printed and bound in Great Britain by
The Bath Press, Bath

To Elizabeth Field
for a decade of devotion

Contents

Notes on Contributors

MONICA ATTIAS has been a member of the Community of Sant'Egidio since 1978. During the last ten years she has been actively involved in the promotion of Christian Unity and the organisation of the international meetings 'Peoples and Religions'. At present, with a team of Community members, she helps in the historical research on the Christian Witnesses of the Twentieth Century. She also works for the Italian weekly magazine *Internazionale*.

PROFESSOR AVERIL CAMERON has been Warden of Keble College, Oxford since 1994 and was formerly Professor of Late Antique and Byzantine Studies at King's College, London. She is a Fellow of the British Academy, the Ecclesiastical History Society and the Society of Antiquaries. She was awarded the CBE in 1999. She is the author of several books, including most recently a new translation and commentary on Eusebius's *Life of Constantine*, published in collaboration with Professor Stuart G. Hall.

THE REVD DR JOSEPH CASSIDY, a Canadian by birth, is Principal of St Chad's College, University of Durham. Prior to that he was Senior Lecturer in Southampton, lecturing in ethics, spirituality and pastoral care. In addition to holding doctorates in philosophy and theology he has received formal training in hospital and prison chaplaincy, and has much experience in spiritual direction and directing retreats. A Jesuit for thirteen years, he left before final vows in 1990 and became an Anglican. He has published numerous articles in ethics and spirituality.

THE REVD STEPHEN CONWAY has been the Chairman of the

Executive of Affirming Catholicism since 1997 and was formerly convenor of the Affirming Catholicism group in the General Synod of the Church of England. He is Senior Chaplain to the Bishop of Durham, having previously served as a parish priest and as a director of ordinands.

THE REVD STEPHEN COTTRELL has just been appointed as Canon Pastor of Peterborough Cathedral. He is also a member of the Springboard team, the Archbishops of York and Canterbury's initiative for evangelism. Before this he was Diocesan Missioner in the Diocese of Wakefield. He has written widely about evangelism, the work of initiation and spirituality. He has published a number of books, and is one of the authors of *Emmaus: The Way of Faith*, a widely used programme for evangelism, nurture and discipleship. He has also written *Catholic Evangelism* in the Affirming Catholicism series.

THE REVD PROFESSOR L. WILLIAM COUNTRYMAN is Sherman E. Johnson Professor in Biblical Studies at The Church Divinity School of the Pacific in Berkeley, California. He was ordained priest in the Diocese of Oklahoma in 1965 and has since served a number of parishes and chaplaincies, and has also taught widely. He writes and speaks on a wide variety of topics ranging from the Bible to gay and lesbian spirituality. His is perhaps best known for *Dirt, Greed and Sex*, a study of sexual ethics in the New Testament and their significance today, and *The Poetic Imagination: An Anglican Spiritual Tradition*.

THE MOST REVD DR ROWAN WILLIAMS became Archbishop of Wales in 1999. Prior to that he was Bishop of Monmouth. He has taught theology at Mirfield, Cambridge and Oxford, where he was Lady Margaret Professor of Divinity. He has been a member of the Doctrine Commission of both the Church of England and the Church in Wales, and was consultant to the last Lambeth Conference. His many publications include, most recently, *Sergii Bulgakov: Towards a Russian Political Theology, On Christian Theology: Collected Essays* and *Lost Icons*.

THE REVD PROFESSOR FRANCES YOUNG has taught Theology at the University of Birmingham since 1971. In 1986 she was elected to the Edward Cadbury Chair. She became Dean of the Faculty of Arts in 1995 and since 1997 has served as Pro-Vice-Chancellor. Her main areas of research have been Patristics and New Testament. In 1984 she was ordained a Methodist minister. Her many publications include *Sacrifice and the Death of Christ, Can These Dry Bones Live?* and *From Nicea to Chalcedon*.

THE RIGHT REVD DAVID STANCLIFFE has been Bishop of Salisbury since 1993, having formerly been Provost of Portsmouth. He has been the Chairman of the Church of England's Liturgical Commission since 1993 and has overseen the preparation and introduction of *Common Worship*. He is currently the President of Affirming Catholicism in the UK and Ireland.

THE RIGHT REVD JACK NICHOLLS has been Bishop of Sheffield since 1997. Before that he was Bishop of Lancaster. He is a well known missioner and spiritual director in the UK.

Foreword

Stephen Conway

The chapters of this book spring from talks and papers delivered by the authors to the tenth anniversary conference of Affirming Catholicism held in Durham in September 2000. In spite of the local difficulty of a British rail crisis, 250 participants from around the Anglican Communion, from the Swedish Lutheran and Roman Catholic Churches gathered for what was intended to be an extended Eucharist, celebrated and explored over four days.

Our speakers were asked to address us very directly and not to come and read papers ready for publication. I am delighted that we have proceeded since the conference to produce this substantial book through the commitment of the contributors. My hope is that as people read the individual chapters they will still be able to discern the passionate and eloquent engagement of speakers and participants during the conference itself.

From the outset the intention of the planning group was that the conference might enable the participants to celebrate our faith in the Incarnation through the prism of the heart of our worship as sacramental Christians. It is entirely in order for our President, David Stancliffe, to draw attention to the shape of the eucharistic rite in his chapter; but the purpose of the conference and now the book is not primarily liturgical. It is to explore how we are formed by the Eucharist as the Church and as members of the Body of Christ. Following St Augustine, we pray that we may become what we eat. As Stancliffe says, first Christ shares our life; and then he changes it.

Taking each component of the Eucharist in turn helps us further to understand the re-presentation of the sacrifice of

Christ in the context of the flourishing and renewal of all creation and enables us better to fathom our part in that sacrifice and flourishing. As Stephen Cottrell reminds us, we need to gather right, honestly acknowledging our humanity and context. Our celebration of the Eucharist, however, is not chiefly a private matter: it places us in solidarity with all God's little ones, and with our enemies as well as our friends within the encompassing mercy of God. Monica Attias reminds us that our confession in the Eucharist means both the outflowing of our penitence and our stand for all the people whom God calls to the divine banquet.

Having recollected ourselves in the presence of the God who has declared in our favour in Christ, we are called to wait upon God's word in the Scriptures. Bill Countryman's work refreshes us both about the nature of the authority of the text over us and about the way in which our liturgical reading of the Scriptures becomes key to the rhythm of all transformation in our lives. This is constantly put to the test as we are invited by God to be agents in the proclamation of transformation in the way that Rowan Williams sets out for us.

Every Sunday and solemnity we proclaim our faith in the words of the Creed. The Eucharist may be celebrated in many styles to meet the needs of pastoral care and mission. Each time we are part of the celebration we pray that we may be made new, both individually and as a community. We do this with confidence because we know that the Eucharist is Christ's gift to the Church from the beginning. Our recitation of the Creed reminds us of the faith and the rich tradition which we have received and of which we are part today. At the same time, Averil Cameron reminds us that the development of the Christian creeds provides us with a paradigm for our journey in faith and gives us pointers to the glorious mystery of God, rather than a blueprint beyond all critical reflection.

Jack Nicholls' chapter on the Prayer of the People calls us to remember that what we are called to do in the Eucharist is not to consider propositions but persons. We come each time to draw close to the person of Christ at Calvary in whom the love of God meets the agony of the world. Here we stay with the world on our hearts, praying that we and all for whom we pray will be transfigured with Christ on the altar of the cross.

The transformation which is proclaimed in the Eucharist and for which we pray is focused in the Great Thanksgiving Prayer, illuminated for us by Frances Young. Here we offer our prayer over bread and wine and invoke the Holy Spirit on the elements and ourselves as we rehearse the drama of creation and redemption. Our heartfelt thanks and praise are expressed for the world, the universe and everything. This is the deepest reality we know. It is as we accept the reality of the world as it is that we offer our hope of the new creation and the completion of all things in Christ.

Renewed by the Eucharist, we embrace again the world groaning in travail, exhorted by our Post Communion Prayer to look for glory and transformation. Joe Cassidy's chapter paints a picture of what truly motivates us into reflection and action as Christians, how we might understand our decision-making, and how we might most effectively integrate our response in service to Christ with emotional intelligence. Included in the volume is an adaptation of Stephen Cottrell's sermon at the final Mass of the Durham conference which reminds us that we must serve our catholic understanding of the gospel of love by learning new tunes in which to sing of God's glory in the world and in Christ Jesus.

I have added a further contribution from Averil Cameron as an Appendix. This was a valued contribution to the previous Affirming Catholicism conference in 1998, which it was not possible to publish elsewhere. Her exposition of the meaning of tradition is an important codicil to all that has gone before it.

The themed nature of this book has meant that it has not been possible to reproduce here the excellent sermons delivered in Durham Cathedral during the conference, nor the meditations at the extended Exposition of the Blessed Sacrament. One of the sermons was preached by The Reverend Angela Tilby, writer, broadcaster and Tutor in Spirituality at Westcott House. The other was preached by The Reverend Dr Johann Dalman, Theological Secretary of the Swedish Lutheran Church. These will both appear in the Affirming Catholicism Newsletter. I thank them both. It is our regret that the Archbishop of Uppsala was prevented from being with us by air traffic control problems but we salute his serious efforts to get through. Our thanks go also to Canon Kate Tristram from Holy Island who acted with Angela as a conference chaplain. My thanks go, too, to Father Stanley Baxter for stepping into the breach. We are grateful to the Dean and Chapter of the Cathedral for their warm hospitality and most particularly thankful for the generous and professional care which we received from the staff of St Chad's and St John's Colleges. All those who attended the conference will want to share with me in expressing gratitude to Perran Gay and Dominic Barrington for all their work in preparation for the conference and its worship. The conference could not have taken place at all without the skill and experience of our Administrator, Elizabeth Field.

I owe a great debt of thanks to all the speakers and contributors to this volume and to Brendan Walsh and his colleagues at DLT. I pray that this book will help readers to understand the Eucharist in fresh ways and live it with joy.

Stephen Conway
Durham, March 2001

Introduction*

David Stancliffe

His kind will always lose in the end. I know this, and now I know why. Whether it's wife or nation they occupy, their mistake is the same: they stand still, and their stake moves underneath them. *The Pharaoh died*, says Exodus, *and the children of Israel sighed by reason of their bondage*. Chains rattle, rivers roll, animals startle and bolt, forests inspire and expand, babies stretch open-mouthed from the womb, new seedlings arch their necks and creep forward into the light. Even a language won't stand still. A territory is only possessed for a moment in time. They stake everything on that moment, posing for photographs while planting the flag, casting themselves in bronze. Washington crossing the Delaware. The capture of Okinawa. They're desperate to hang on. But they can't.

These are the words of a wife and mother, who went with her Baptist missionary husband and her family of girls to a remote place in the Belgian Congo. In the end, her husband's *idées fixes* about the Congo's darkness, his rightness and everyone else's wrongness, makes it all unravel. And to hear the Genesis, Revelation, Judges, Exodus and the Song of the Three Children you must read Barbara Kingsolver's remarkable novel, *The Poisonwood Bible*.

But for now it is his wife Orleanna, not Nathan the preacher, who has grasped the essential truth. She has come to realise, slowly and painfully, that his religion is wrong. His religion is always right, and he is always right, so it cannot – he cannot – engage with anyone or anything; not the Congolese, nor the country, nor his family, not even himself. And at last she realises that this must be wrong;

that a prison of absolute fixity is not how we or anything living grows. A seed meets soil and water and warmth, and grows. We meet people and learn from them, and in that meeting we are changed, we come alive, we grow.

What Orleanna has last discovered is the basic truth of the Christian faith, the truth that we approach, embrace, are changed by and inspired by each time we celebrate the Eucharist. At its heart our Eucharist is not a thing, a statement, a philosophical construct. It is a process, God-given, which catches us up, and then transforms us. In this way, it mirrors exactly the two things that God does for us in Jesus Christ: first, he shares our life; then he changes it.

The grand words for sharing our life and then changing it, which give this simple theorem theological respectability, are incarnation and redemption. And as Gregory Nazianzus was clear, you cannot have redemption without incarnation first. 'That which God did not assume, he did not redeem.' What is important here is to stress the directness of God's engagement with his people. You can read the Old Testament as a long story of God's attempts to gain a response to his gift of conscious life, with all the freedoms and pitfalls that has brought to his people. There was the covenant with Noah and Abraham; there was the rescue from Egypt and the giving of the Commandments; there was the establishment of the Davidic kingdom and its failures; there was the Exile and the rebuilding of Jerusalem – all attempts to engage with the creatures he had made in his image and entrusted with the potential for responsive love. But in the end, they did not hear. In spite of valiant attempts by the prophets to make it as vivid as they could, it was not direct speech. As the letter to the Hebrews says, 'In former times God spoke to our forebears in many and various ways through the prophets.' But now there was only one way left: face to face engagement. 'In these last days he has spoken to us by his Son, whom he appointed heir of all things, through whom he created the worlds' (Heb. 1:1–2).

An example of how the gospel writers consciously reflect the cost of this enormous risk is the parable of the Wicked Tenants in Mark 12, where the vineyard owner is finally driven to sending his son, saying 'They will respect my son.' But the fact remains that however risky, there is nothing like face to face engagement. We can write each other letters or send all the e-mails in the world, but it is only face to face that encounter can be guaranteed to change people. People may not hear each other aright, but there's always a chance to correct misleading impressions and false assumptions when you see what reaction you get. For a meeting to be real, there must be dialogue and response, and that means both must speak and both must listen.

It is something of this mutuality, this interchange, that is implied in John's image of the Divine Word pitching his tent in our midst. And if we were tempted to think that this was only a more efficient way of God making his personal megaphone more inescapably present, we have only to contrast the gospel writers' account of the ministry of Jesus with the style of the prophets in the Old Testament. It is the prepositions that indicate the change. Whereas the prophets of old spoke *at* people, and delivered their uncompromising take-it-or-leave-it messages, Jesus speaks *with* people, and asks them questions. He is searching for a response, for dialogue. 'I am *among* you as one who serves' is the motto for engagement of a God who shares our life, and is serious about the conversation.

And why is he serious? Because dialogue leads to growth and change, and without such a dialogue his people cannot grow up and become themselves. And if God is looking for a response to the initiative of his love, he knows that has to be a free, unconditional offer. The excitement for us is that when we trust that offer, we find that the meeting unlocks responses we did not know we were capable of deep within us. Engagement with a God who listens, and draws out of you what you have to give, is a life-changing experience. Each time we meet, further scales drop from our eyes, more of our pretentious defences shatter, and in our vulnerability we seem not so much broken as healed. This is because engagement leads to change, just as incarnation, always a risk, leads to the cross and redemption.

This is not just something that once happened; though happen it did. It is a pattern that has been consciously repeated in history, and found to be true. It is true to God,

3

because that is the pattern of his dealings with us: in Jesus he first shares our life, then he changes it. And if this pattern is good enough for God, it should be good enough for us. It is a pattern that is true of our basic human experience about how we grow up, about what happens when we meet other people, and it is this divinely appointed and utterly practical pattern that we place ourselves within and form ourselves around each time we assemble to celebrate the Eucharist. That is, after all, what we were taught to do by Jesus to make it all happen, so we shouldn't be surprised.

How catholic is this view of the Eucharist? As the Durham Conference testified, there is a longing to make the connections between what we do in church and how we live the faith we proclaim. The variety of the contributions certainly attests our catholicity, and the conference modelled a pattern of ecclesial unity which is very Anglican. We believe in unity, not uniformity, and we draw our model from the tradition we find in 1 Corinthians 12 and Acts 2, where unity within the body is discovered to be the rich harmony of complementary diversity rather than the flat unison of an imposed uniformity.

This rediscovery of the nature of our unity is important for our understanding of the significance of the eucharistic action, where the scattered fragments of our lives are made whole, and the extraordinary collection of broken humanity, invited to his feast from the hedgerows and byways by a God who is always seeking fresh ways of including us in when we try and make the gates of his Church too narrow, find themselves seated together at his table. But it is also important for what we used to call catholic social action. If the Eucharist is the offering and consecration of our common life, then what are we bringing to God for his blessing? What part are we playing in forming not just a new identity for the catholic tradition in the Church of England, but a new identity for the community as a whole?

The country of which we are citizens (as we have learnt to be in this bright new age where citizenship has replaced our being subjects of the Crown) could do worse than take the process of engagement and transformation as the key

4

to a new way of exploring life together. If it is indeed a God-given pattern for our life together, ought we not to share it as widely as we can, instead of just keeping it as a way of being Church? For although you might not think it, it is the world that God came to save, not the Church.

1 The Gathering Rite*

Stephen Cottrell

The purpose of the Gathering Rite in the Eucharist is that the People of God might be gathering right. The purpose of the rite is that we might be constituted as the Body of Christ: that we might gather right, knowing who we are, what we are about and where we are going. When I am teaching children about the Eucharist, either as part of preparation for Communion or in church schools, I usually say to them that if you want to understand what the Eucharist is about, then you must remember the three kisses. There are three kisses in the Eucharist, and this helps us to understand both the theology and the practice of the Mass.

Liturgically speaking, the Eucharist begins with the president kissing the altar. In fact, in the church where I worship, St Thomas' Huddersfield, occasionally the whole of the worshipping community kisses the altar during the opening hymn as a sign that we are the priestly people of God. The reason we kiss the altar is because the altar is a place of encounter. We have come together, as the people of God, in order that we might meet and encounter Jesus. And on that altar, in breaking and sharing bread and wine, we are going to encounter the Lord. The next kiss comes when the deacon, having proclaimed the word of God, kisses the book of the gospels. This kiss is offered again to signify that the word of God is a place of encounter with Jesus Christ.

Recognising that each of our neighbours is also a powerful focus of encounter with Jesus, we kiss each other as a sign of Peace. This comes at a beguiling point in the

*© Stephen Cottrell 2000

liturgy. I do not think that the Liturgical Commission really picked up on this, because the thing about the Anglican position for the Peace is that everybody from the Church of England goes into intermission mode. We get up, have a stretch and look for our change. There is a collection coming up any minute. Notwithstanding this practice and the hope of being nice to one another, we are actually greeting one another and celebrating the encounter with Jesus which comes from our being the Body of Christ together. There is a sense in which the Jesus in me reaches out to acknowledge and greet the Jesus in you.

I am convinced that these three kisses vividly illustrate a full-blooded catholic understanding of the Mass. So I said to my three small sons, 'Remember the three kisses. Remember those three encounters with Jesus, and you will have a pretty good idea what the Eucharist is about.' I trust that they may have taken this in, but there is little direct evidence of their having done so. Conversations that we have at home before we go to Mass on Sunday mornings are more likely to begin with a question like, 'Is it alright if I take this gun with me?' Not a real gun of course . . . Or, 'Can I take my Pokemon cards' or, 'Will it be boring and how long will it be?'

The point I want to demonstrate through my children's questions is that we may all have a very good theology of the Eucharist; but when we arrive as the People of God to worship, all of us are coming from different situations in which we are encountering conflicts and tensions in our lives. Most of us are sitting there in those first few minutes as worship begins, and our minds are not on worship. We are trying to keep our children somehow under control; we are trying to reassure them that the service will not be boring. Many of us will arrive having had a big argument over the decision to come to church at all. The very fact that we come to church is often a source of conflict and tension within families, and certainly within our culture. There are other challenges: our culture has so many more interesting things to offer us to do on Sunday mornings than used to be the case.

It is so important to emphasise for ourselves that the point of the Gathering Rite is that we should gather right.

7

The point of those first few moments in the liturgy is first gently to acknowledge the tensions and frustrations and difficulties people have in getting to church at all. Then we begin to prepare and raise people's hearts and minds to the knowledge and expectation that they are going to see the face of Christ. They are going to meet Jesus in broken bread and in poured wine. They are going to hear Jesus speaking to them through his word, and they are going to find, love and cherish Jesus in the motley band of people around them. Therefore, although the Gathering Rite itself consists of just a few things, like kissing the altar, greeting the people, a prayer of preparation, a penitential rite, together they are a kind of set prayer that we go through to prepare ourselves. I think this is one of the points within the liturgy where it is appropriate for the person who is presiding to depart from the text and to gather people in. The president might do this by acknowledging what is happening in the world, and by making some connections between the liturgy and the lives that we are seeking to live. The point of the Gathering Rite is that we gather right, that we prepare our hearts to meet and encounter Jesus. Because I believe that is the point of those three kisses and those three encounters, I cannot actually think of a better way of explaining the Eucharist to anybody, child or adult. I want people when they come to Mass to know and be ready with eager and expectant hearts that they are going to see and find Jesus in what they are doing.

The wonderful truth about that encounter is that when we look for Jesus in the liturgy or in any form of prayer we are going to be surprised by what we find. He is never quite as we expected. We are able to conjure many images of Jesus in our own imagination. These images are fed by the images created by others, many of which were displayed together in the most startlingly evocative Millennium event, the *Seeing Salvation* exhibition in the National Gallery in Trafalgar Square in London. For me, however, the most powerful Millennium image of Christ was a statue. It is the statue, *Ecce Homo*, by Mark Wallinger which for six months was on the so-called empty plinth in Trafalgar Square, outside the National Gallery. Apparently, that plinth in Trafalgar Square has been empty for 158 years. Successive government committees had sought to decide what to put on the empty plinth, but those involved could never make up their minds, until someone had the bright idea of a Millennium project.

In September 1999, this statue was raised onto the plinth for a six-month sojourn in Trafalgar Square. They do say that if you hang around Trafalgar Square long enough you will meet everybody. For a while, visitors encountered this statue of Christ as a temporary lodger. Imagine yourself in Trafalgar Square for a minute. The other statues in the Square are very interesting, of course. Pre-eminent stands Nelson on his column. We will not dwell on the symbolism of this! Around him are those great, giant lions. In the other three corners of the square are General Charles James Napier, George IV on horseback and Sir Henry Havelock. These great figures, cast in bronze, are absolutely massive, three or four or five times larger than life. These dimensions make it all the more shocking that the image of Christ is only life-size and, by comparison, incredibly small.

Jesus is perched precariously on the edge of this huge plinth, and he looks ordinary and vulnerable and lost and very, very human. His shaven head echoes for us images of Kosovo, or Belsen or Auschwitz. His bewildered expression does not seem to invest the horror with any meaning. He seems just another ordinary innocent, caught up in something bigger than himself. His barbed wire crown of thorns is made out of gold but it looks slightly camp.

On the day that the statue was unveiled various daily newspapers sent reporters into Trafalgar Square to interview passers-by about what they thought of the statue, and I record here some of their very interesting responses. Somebody said: 'You couldn't put your faith in someone like that, he's as weak as a kitten.' And this is a very interesting one: 'His smallness just shows what little meaning Christianity has in today's world.' I love this one: 'He's a typically lily-livered, Anglican Jesus.' Somebody else said, 'I just want to go up there and give him a hug. I never notice the other statues in the square, they are just target practice for pigeons, but he looks so vulnerable, you just want to take him home.'

The motivation of the artist, Mark Wallinger, is all the

Mark Wallinger, *Ecce Homo*, 1999. Life size. Installed in Trafalgar Square, London.
© The Artist, courtesy Anthony Reynolds Gallery, London.

more interesting for his not being a Christian. He was asked to create any statue he liked to put on this plinth. His reasoning was that it was the Millennium, which must have something to do with the birth of Jesus Christ. The obvious subject matter for the statue, therefore, was a figure of Jesus. It is interesting that it took somebody from outside of the Church to have that basic confidence and faith to do something Christian to mark the Millennium. He said: 'I wanted to show Christ as an ordinary human being, led out in front of a lynch mob, and I think he has a place here, in front of all these over-sized, imperial symbols.' Some of the criticism of this statue came from Christians. Some Christians thought he looked 'too human, too ordinary'. I thought this was interesting: 'Neither heroic, nor heroically fragile.' 'He expresses both the presence of Christ, and the question that this new Millennium poses – who, exactly, is Jesus Christ? Is he the treasure for whom I would willingly forsake everything? Is he the yeast that would transform the world? Or is he just another lost innocent, stripped now even of the meaning that the last two millennia have invested?'

What is disturbing for us as we look at this image of Christ, is that this is how many people today see Jesus. There is not much God left in him. At the same time, however, this is also the Christ I long to discover. It is the Christ who bewilders and surprises me, the embarrassingly human Christ, not the Christ I was expecting, not the image of God that I would have drawn. And his brief epiphany in Trafalgar Square is for me a reminder of God's persistence. Here is God in Jesus Christ, standing in the breach between vanity and sacrifice. It is neither pretty nor heroic. It is just the logical end of loving, and there is nothing to be said. Can we see the face of God in such a very human, very vulnerable Christ, this victim, this about-to-be-broken Christ?

If we do see God in such a figure of Christ, we are astonished. He is still here, after all these years, still among us, and how embarrassing that is to our sophisticated selves. He is still wearing that twisted crown of thorns that we placed on his head when we wanted to get rid of him. He just does not seem to get the joke. It seemed like we were managing so well without him, but trust him to come back with such a vulgar show of humility.

I believe this is a measure of how Jesus comes to us, finds us and works on us in the liturgy. He comes to us if we gather right, and if our hearts are ready, to confound us and to bewilder us. We gather for the Eucharist, tired and frustrated and bored by what our lives have become; and our expectations are all but dried up. And then his word is broken open to us. Words of promise and absolution are spoken to us. Bread and wine are given to us, and we behold him. We behold him in the tiny frailty of the broken bread, we hear him speaking to us through his word, and our hearts are stirred to find him, and to minister to him in the world. We begin to do that very strange something that you cannot define or pin down. We begin to worship. The point of the Gathering Rite is to gather right, with expectant hearts to meet the Jesus who is expecting us.

2 Reconciliation and the Eucharist – Heart and World*

Monica Attias

I am delighted by this opportunity to write about the reconciliation work of our community and about reconciliation work in general. I am not writing from an academically theological point of view, but rather from the perspective of one who sees reconciliation as a lifelong commitment, as a Christian and as a member of the Community of Sant'Egidio.

I begin with the words of St John Chrysostom about reconciliation. He pointed out four ways to live out reconciliation. The first way is the condemnation of our own sins, quoting from Psalm 32: 'I made my sin known to you, and you, for your own part took away my sin.' So condemn your sins, and this is sufficient for the Lord for your liberation, and it is sufficient for you to become more prudent and not to fall into sin again. Second, he asserts equally powerfully: 'Do not remember the failings of your enemies. Control your anger. Pardon the brothers and sisters who hurt you. If you forgive others their failings your Heavenly Father will forgive yours' (Matt. 6). The third way of purification which he urges upon his readers is fervent prayer well done, that comes from deep within the heart. Fourth, 'If you want to know a fourth way I will tell you, this is almsgiving and it has a great value.'

It is very beautiful to begin with these ancient words, because I think that in our contemporary world, where the presence of God is often not perceived anymore and where speaking about sin seems out of date, these words can seem too radical and too simple. Yet all these words are contained in the prayer of Our Father, which is also the prayer of brotherhood and sisterhood. All of us need to be forgiven by God and by our sisters and brothers. All of us need to forgive in our turn.

I would like to start from the Scriptures with the story of two brothers. At the origin of the world and of humanity, in the very first pages of the Bible, after the first murder in history, the Lord asks Cain a question: 'Where is your brother Abel?' This same question resounds across the centuries, and it reaches us today, 'Where is your brother Abel?' It is a question addressed to all men and women of all generations and it means, where is your brother and where is your sister who are suffering? Where are your brother and your sister, who speak a different language? Where are your brother and your sister who are sick or poor? It is a question to all men and women who forget about others because they are focused on themselves, concerned primarily for their own good. Such selfishness is not confined to individuals. The question is also posed to dominant groups within societies and to all the rich countries of the world.

This question is at the root of reconciliation. Yet, sadly, the most common answer remains that of Cain. Cain is not the most evil man in the world, he is simply the one who, in following his nature, cares for his own interests. It is the answer of Cain: 'Am I my brother's keeper?' – what do I have to do with him? Why should I care? I have to think about myself. The rivalry of siblings is a theme which recurs throughout the Bible. Care for one's own interests always transforms the brother first into a stranger and then into an enemy to be feared and defeated. The Scriptures are very clear: recognising others as brothers and sisters does not come naturally. Only in the Lord can we find reconciliation with our brothers and sisters.

In the New Testament Jesus challenges the question still more. He asks us to consider even our enemies as brothers. Following the example of Jesus recorded in John 13, at the Lord's Supper we learn to be servants and to wash one another's feet. Our being bonded more deeply into the family of Jesus through our participation in the Lord's

Supper is, therefore, the first and decisive step towards reconciliation. It is the first conscious step towards recognising others as brothers and sisters. The Eucharist, then, is at the root of our sympathy for our contemporaries wherever they are to be found and in whatever circumstances. The Sacrament generates an attitude of respect and closeness, of such a degree of participation in the hopes and anguishes of our neighbours that everyone can say, 'Yes, I am my brother's keeper', and everyone can say, 'Yes, I am my brother's servant'. God's earnest call to Christians is that we seek the grace to redeem Cain's answer through a new culture of solidarity, through a fresh conception of the mutuality of relationship. We need to be reconciled with others through a joyful and deeply heartfelt affirmation of a theology of otherness and difference.

We need to understand with our hearts and with our souls that there is more joy in giving than in receiving. And here I would like to reflect for one moment on the way of thought that St John Chrysostom pointed out: almsgiving. Almsgiving has become in recent years in Italy an almost forbidden word, as if giving to the poor was always and inevitably a way of prolonging their poverty. I recognise the contentiousness of the issue, but it is certainly true that for centuries almsgiving has been the only contact between the world of the rich and the world of the poor, the only contact between a rich person and a poor person. This is a direct form of contact which is being lost. We are afraid of a personal encounter with the poor, even if it is only for giving some money. I repeat there are many ways to look at this question, but we are definitely losing that small contact which is almsgiving, which is already a little sign of reconciliation, already a little sign of friendship. So the challenge for the Church is not that of being well-organised, or to provide good social services or just to be efficient. Service has to be first of all a sign of reconciliation, an answer to the Lord's question, 'Where is your brother?' A friendly presence next to a man or a woman who is suffering is not just to be considered social activity. A presence that can console, that can accompany and heal is not social service. It is something much more profound than that. It is friendship, it is deep brotherhood and sisterhood.

15

Christians are not primarily called to organise services to the poor, they are called to begin to answer the question of the Lord by saying, 'Yes, I am indeed my brothers' and my sisters' servant.' The service of the poor is not primarily a work but the vocation of the Christian. It is a redemptive and reconciling turning upside-down of the logic of division that caused the death of Abel.

The love of self to the exclusion of others is the root of violence. And Christians are not destined either to live in the indifference and violence of Cain or to tolerate it as any kind of norm in human society. To combat such assumptions we need, therefore, to build up a new culture of reconciliation. The challenge of the Church today is to give new soul to our western world, and to reconcile the divisions which still persist at the beginning of this new millennium. It is my contention that this is the key issue today, and it touches all aspects of our lives, the spiritual and personal, as well as the life of all nations, and eventually of the world itself. War, the most striking example of the failure of men and women to find the true way to reconciliation, is an ever-present reality. War in Africa, the Gulf, the Middle East and the Balkans in recent years and up to this very day suggests that warfare and violence are simply uncontrollable. The naive hopes generated in 1989, after the collapse of the Berlin Wall, are long gone. War has grown even to touch Europe, a continent free of wars between nations since 1945. In 1989 more than 35 states were involved in conflicts and civil wars. Between 1990 and 1994 war involved 50 countries.

For all the technology and double-speak of modern warfare, it is not a computer game without consequences. The human cost of war is devastating in lives lost, homes and livelihoods destroyed and land polluted. From 1990 to 1994 the number of refugees grew from 39 to 47 million. It is always the people in the greatest need and with the least freedom who suffer most. It would seem, however, that even those who control the weapons of mass destruction and claim the expertise in diplomacy are powerless before the obstinacy of conflict. No one seems to hold the key to peace any more. On the contrary, it seems as if on a daily basis a ritual of powerlessness is celebrated and portrayed

16

on our television screens in a parade of the images of war, violence and tragedy.

Where does the responsibility for all this lie? Who holds the keys to effective reconciliation in Burundi, Rwanda, Sudan, Sierra Leone, East Timor or Kosovo? Whether on the inside of the conflict or looking in from the outside, it is difficult today to understand what has been happening in these countries. Or rather, it is difficult to accept all of this without giving a too easy explanation: it is your fault . . . it is the other's fault, it is the fault of fundamentalism. In the face of this death-dealing lazy thinking there is a strong temptation for Christians to join the chorus of 'there is nothing we can do'. It is true that in some cases there is very little that can be done practically, but hopelessness is never the condition of Christians. We may be powerless in front of the final revelation of evil embodied in the fact of war and the inhumanity of humans; but we do have the power of changing our heart, and this makes a big difference. We do have the power of changing our hearts, and uprooting the roots of evil and violence that are within us, because violence and war find a good ground in our hearts.

A convert from Judaism to Romanian Orthodoxy, Nicu Steinhardt, wrote a luminous book about passing through the trial of communist prisons entitled, *A Journal of Happiness*. 'I always get very angry', he says, 'when I see how Christianity is confused with stupidity, with a kind of idiotic and cowardly devotion, as if the destiny of Christianity is nothing else but to let humanity be cheated by the power of evil. Many say that Christianity itself helps such wickedness, because, by definition it is condemned to blindness and paralysis.' This reflection touches the very root of a great choice which Christianity had to make during the twentieth century: whether to face up to the complexity of human life, confronting the powers of evil, or the other choice, to dilute the radical message of the Gospel. As Steinhardt says, 'The great temptation has been to live, letting evil cheat us, with acceptance and resignation.'

It is an attitude that we still find in front of the great tragedies of today's world. What can we do? The global media give us a great deal of information about the evil being done; but we are paralysed by the burden of the knowledge. Sometimes the Christian faith feared weakness and tried to find strength somewhere else, in power. All religions had this temptation. This generated a cult for power under many forms: money, armed force and so on. The great problem of religious fundamentalism today finds its roots here. Its roots are in the search of the strength of the religion, rather than the vulnerable strength of faith. The twin temptations to power or resignation can and should be resisted. We have the testimony of our forebears in faith to prove it. The Chief Rabbi of Romania during the Second World War, Alexandre Safran, struggled with all his strength against the Nazi threat to deport the Jewish people of his country. His biographer, Jean Ancel, writes: 'His life is an extraordinary example of a fight without weapons, without bombs, with only the resource of the strength of the spirit, opposed to brutal force. It is the story of a disarmed strength, aimed at reconciling men and women, making them more merciful, transforming them from within.'

The operation of vulnerable strength is also to be discovered in the experience of other people around the world during the century we have just left. These were people inspired by faith and far from resignation who were able to generate change, while seeking detachment from all temptation to power and vengeful violence. In 1960, Martin Luther King, speaking about his pilgrimage towards non-violence, said: 'In the midst of the dangers that surround me, I felt at peace, and I have experienced those resources of strength only God can give. In many cases I felt the power of God transform the strain of despair into the happiness of hope.' This is the discovery of that vulnerable strength which is common to life-bearing religious paths and which was exhibited so wonderfully in the witness of the Mahatma in India, not only in his non-violent pursuit of freedom and justice for a new India after colonial rule but also in his love for the Untouchables and his giving them hope and value. Wherever such voices have been heard, the accent is always upon finding ways to affirm reconciliation, instead of confrontation. For some, like King and Gandhi, it was a voice for which they were prepared to die to keep being heard. 'Peace is waiting for its prophets', said Pope John Paul II to the gathering of leaders of world faiths at Assisi, and he continued, 'Together we have filled our eyes with visions of peace. They radiate the energies for a new language of peace, for new signs of peace. These must be signs that will break the fatal chains of the divisions inherited from history, and generated by modern ideologies. This peace is waiting for its artisans. Peace is a worksite open to all, and not only to the specialists, the wise and the strategists.' Peace, on these terms, is the vocation of every Christian: it is neither just for the diplomats nor for the strategists; it is the challenge of every Christian person.

I can only explain further what I mean by telling you something about the experience of how the Community of Sant'Egidio has tried to lead this vocation to reconciliation. The pursuit of reconciliation through the Eucharist has always been the core of our spiritual experience. The Community of Sant'Egidio was founded in 1968 by Andrea Riccardi, who was then a high school student in Rome. A group of students gathered to read the Gospel, and to exchange views about their city, searching for what it all meant to their lives. It was a time of turmoil during the student troubles which swept Europe and America in the late 1960s. It was a time of great discussion in Europe and the United States when the old values were increasingly being questioned. There was a big desire to change the world. Andrea and his friends decided to take a particular path, wanting to follow the Gospel and to befriend the poor. You cannot love Jesus in the Blessed Sacrament and not find him and love him in the poor whom he came to save. Coming from wealthy families themselves, the Community members felt all the more strongly that the presence of so many poor people in the city of Rome and in the world was a compelling issue. Over the years, the Community has seen the different faces of poverty, without limiting itself by specialising in one particular area of need, like children or the elderly. From the beginning, the Community has tried to keep an open heart, and to see people's needs as they arose. This has made the Community aware

19

of many different groups who experience poverty and discrimination: the old, the disabled, the homeless, foreign immigrants, those living with AIDS and gypsies. Today the friendship of the Community embraces many other countries. We take care of a hospital in Guinea Bissau in Africa. We work in the prisons of many African cities. We have been working in refugee camps with the Kosovar victims of war. Most of all, friendship with the poor in a world that teaches that all should be self-sufficient has represented the greatest blessing in our history as a Community. Meeting the weakness of the poor has helped us discover the true meaning of being human and being Christian. The lie of self-sufficiency is revealed in our being wholly dependent upon God and not on our own strength. In the Eucharist we are all beggars together at the heavenly banquet.

Besides the student tumult over the crisis of democracy in 1968, the major influence upon the development of the Community was the Second Vatican Council which ended in 1965. The Council outlined a new path for the Roman Catholic Church in the contemporary world. It sought to return to the roots of the Church, the Gospel, and at the same time, to open a path of empathy with contemporary men and women. The opening text of the Council's document on the Church in the modern world, *Gaudium et Spes*, talks of this empathy and reconciliation with the world. It highlights the joy and the hope, the sadness and the anguish of all the people of today, especially of the poor which must find an echo in the hearts of all who are genuinely human. Following this lead, the path of the Community is to live through our times and to deal with today's problems under the conditions prevailing in modern society. We are ordinary people who make up a largely lay community, who believe that it is possible, even in our contemporary world, to live the Gospel in a radical way, praying together, serving the poor together, and working for peace and reconciliation. We seek to live a brotherhood and sisterhood which is deep, anchored in the glory of worship and that discovery of our true humanity in the Incarnation of Christ which is at the heart of our eucharistic celebration.

We are not a movement in the sense that there are people who come and go. As a community we are a stable family whose members know each other, even though today the Community has around thirty thousand members around the world in a whole variety of countries and situations, from the United States to Rwanda, where we have a community of Hutus and Tutsis living together. In that particularly special setting very practical reconciliation is taking place. The Community gathers young Hutus and Tutsis together to pray. Their breaking bread together finds practical expression in their service to the children who lost their parents during the genocide. It is not easy for them to live as brothers and sisters, of course, but by going back to the root of their lives, the Gospel, they can find this strength.

The Community in Rome meets every night for prayer in the Basilica of Santa Maria in Trastevere in the historical centre of Rome, and also in a number of other churches. On Saturdays we celebrate the Eucharist. This is the source and wellspring of our joy and our service, the banquet to which our Lord invites the poor and the rich and through which he loves all by his standards not ours. Every Christmas Day we have a lunch in the Basilica for more than 500 people. The Community actually pioneered what has become a common practice at Christmas in Rome to fill the Basilica with tables for hospitality. The churches open the doors, and they invite the poor people to come and eat in the church. It is a banquet of reconciliation, and I will always remember what a homeless person said once, 'If someone asked me how heaven will be, I think it will be like this.' This is truly a banquet of reconciliation, the poor and the rich together, sitting around the table of Jesus.

In the opening rite of the Eucharist we confess our sins, having confidence only in the mercy of God to reconcile us to himself. In the Eucharist we show forth the promise revealed in the Gospel of John that, in Christ, God is reconciling the world to himself and that we share in this work of reconciliation. This has opened up for the Community another aspect of reconciliation in its spiritual adventure, the reconciliation of enemies. On 4 October 1992, the peace agreement between the guerrilla fighters and the Marxist

21

government of Mozambique was signed in Rome through the mediation of the Community of Sant'Egidio. A journalist from the *Washington Post* asked Andrea Riccardi, the founder of the Community, when had the Community decided to give up its work with the poor and to work with diplomacy? Andrea answered that we had never stopped working with the poor to become official diplomats because building peace and work with the poor are one and the same. This is very important in our spirituality. The struggle against poverty leads us to struggle against war, the mother of all poverty. A young person that visits an elderly person works for reconciliation as much as the mediator works for peace between two factions in conflict. Reconciliation is at the root of both dimensions of our community life, and the story of our work with Mozambique is a very simple one. A bishop from Mozambique knew one of the priests of the Community, and at the time of famine asked for help. We started to send cargoes and later initiated development projects. It dawned on the Community as it became involved in the life of ordinary Mozambiquans that one of the roots of their continuing poverty was an armed conflict which had lasted since before the end of colonial rule. One million had died and there were two million refugees and still the western world did nothing about it because Mozambique was not a powerful country with many exploitable resources. The Community decided to contact both the guerrillas and the government. Both sides were invited to come together around the table of Sant'Egidio – a table also used for the poor at Christmas. I personally remember the first words that Andrea said to the two factions: 'Let us recognise each other as brothers, part of the same nation.' He spoke of Joseph and his brothers in the Old Testament and told the story of their reconciliation. Little by little we worked on a personal basis with them to find a way to reconciliation.

Our common life is animated by the mystery of forgiveness and reconciliation manifested in the eucharistic action. This life teaches us that a religious faith that does not develop a theology of the other, a theology of reconciliation, is not credible. Sant'Egidio has over the years animated a pilgrimage of people coming from different religious traditions, Jewish, Christian, Muslim, Hindu and Buddhist. It is not a crusade of religions against secularism or modernity. Rather it wants to be the celebration of an important aspect of peace, that is the ability to live at the same time with a convinced identity and also a fraternal dialogue with the secularised world. In 1986, different religious leaders from all over the world got together to pray in Assisi. They were not there to discuss, but to pray. In the framework of the division of the two blocks, West and East, the intuition of the Pope was simple and basic: let the religions abide alongside one another with neither syncretism nor hatred but genuine respect. The Community of Sant'Egidio has carried on this initial intuition of Assisi. We believe passionately in the strength of the peace that is present in the depths of each religious tradition, even if in each case it has been true that in the experience of religions in history there have been seasons in which this value was either ignored or profaned. It is only by going to the depths of one's own religious tradition that one can retrieve the sacred value of peace. When we share the peace in the Eucharist, we acknowledge that this is Christ's peace and is a foretaste of what relationship is like in heaven. Any apprehension of the sacred value of peace demands that we receive it as sheer gift. This disarms the heart and educates for peace, peace that will last.

A good example of this arises out of one particular experience of the major clash between Christianity and Islam. No one could claim that dialogue is not often difficult, but we believe that dialogue is always better than confrontation, and sometimes we have seen little results, not in the short term, but in the long term. A few years ago we invited one of the Islamic leaders of Sudan to come to Sant'Egidio. The dialogue with him was very difficult but he had accepted our invitation and at least it was a contact, an open door. A few years later, some Catholic nuns working in Sudan made an appeal to the Community because their church was just about to be knocked down by the government. On receipt of the appeal, we used that contact from years before. We sought to convince the authorities that we should keep this church and school, that it was important for the people. The approach worked.

23

It was a very small breakthrough but one which was monumentally unexpected. There is no evidence that the overall policy had changed but that man had been changed by our having had dialogue together. This was enough for him to take a fresh step. The delightfully unexpected outcome taught us afresh that such human encounter can only bring good.

In its 32 year history, the Community of Sant'Egidio has tried not to give up in the face of division and the power of evil. From the beginning, the vulnerable strength of the Community is located in the poor. The Community really has to thank the poor for all that they have taught us so far. Our school of faith and humanity has been the shanty town, the inner city, and all the places where the poor people are suffering. Each place has been hallowed by the real presence of Jesus in broken bread and broken lives. It is in these settings that we discover the true character of Christian strength. Great energies spring out from this apparent weakness in which powerful resources are hidden. In the poor we have learned not to avoid weakness but to find endurance and hope. This is what the apostle Paul writes to the Corinthians, 'when I am weak, then I am strong'. So at the beginning of this new century, and this new millennium, every Christian is called to find the courage to be a seed of reconciliation. Such a courage does not come from the wealth we have or from the power we have. Take no gold, nor silver, nor copper in your bags. The courage comes from the love of God. You received without pay, give without pay. With this courage granted to us we will be able to walk on the roads of the world, healing the sick, raising the dead, cleansing the lepers and chasing out our demons of violence and war.

3 The Liturgy of the Word*

L. William Countryman

The liturgical theme of this book prompts us to look at a particularly important aspect of the Anglican approach to Scripture – the way in which the Bible, for us, is embedded in liturgy.[1] The reading of Scripture takes up a significant part of our worship. It is surrounded with a certain reverence and ceremony. It shapes the language of prayer. In the Eucharist, a sermon follows, which often serves to exegete what has been read and bring it into the present. By long tradition, which I want to borrow here, the sermon itself begins with an invocation of the Holy Trinity, that unfathomable Mystery of the divine life that has created all things through an uncontainable and irrepressible love and invites our love in return – love for the divine Trinity and love for all whom the Trinity loves. To God, the Lover, the Beloved and the Love who holds all together in one, be ascribed all praise and worship, now and forever. Amen.

God as Mystery

Appealing to the Trinity here is not only an expression of piety. It also has the practical purpose of reminding us all not to expect too much clarity in what is to follow. I do not claim that the mystery of Anglicanism and the Bible is as elusive or unfathomable as the mystery of the Godhead. But I would claim that all Christian faith has an element of this mystery in it and that, therefore, every faithful and catholic understanding of Christian faith – every faithful and catholic expression of it – always has about it a quality of deliberate restraint or reserve, an acknowledgement of how little we truly know. All theological reflection needs to be grounded in our awareness that God is never within our control, practical or theoretical. The highest insight into God that we can hope to attain, however vivid and seemingly clear, is still only a dim apprehension of the Holy One.

I don't take this as a counsel of despair. It is rather a caution and an encouragement. It cautions us not to become too attached to our favorite stories and images and ideas about God and God's will toward us. No one Christian tradition can rightly claim to have a perfect account of God – nor, for that matter, can all the Christian traditions put together. However convinced we are of our clever formulations, we must remember that, at best, they are only the hem of God's garment. They are not God. To imagine otherwise is the sin of idolatry, which is, of course, the supreme and ever present temptation of the religious. Anglicans have long suspected some of our co-religionists of committing the sin of idolatry in the way they treat the Scriptures; for Fundamentalists, the Bible seems to be virtually interchangeable with God. But how and why is our own approach different?

We are not, after all, innocent. We have our forms of idolatry, too. To judge by our favourite jokes or by the more withering portrayals of us in literature, we tend toward idolatry of liturgy, of good manners, and of the kind of small-scale, local, comfortable tradition that we call 'the way things are done around here'. Well, yes. No religious tradition is free from idolatry. The best any of us can do is to pursue the grace of conversion, to pray for that moment when we can see our idolatries for what they are. But to hope for conversion means accepting the possibility, even the probability of surprise. Things will turn out to be somewhat different from what we supposed. Even if our central affirmations of faith are absolutely true and on target, it will turn out that we haven't really understood them all that well. The experience of surprise and conversion breeds – or at least ought to breed – a certain theological humility.

And such a humility expresses itself in a certain reserve, a certain restraint, a certain reticence in our speech about God. It means claiming less than we would like for our human grasp of God.

The best we can do is to touch the hem of God's garment. But that isn't necessarily so bad. As you will recall, there was a certain woman, once, who suffered a haemorrhage for 12 years, and she found that merely touching that hem was enough to restore her to robust good health.[2] The glory, that is to say the power and beauty, of God is not limited by our weakness. There is encouragement, therefore, in the counsel that we should not expect too much clarity. It is the encouragement that tells us, 'However far you have come, there is still more. The riches of God's life are inexhaustible even to God – how much more to you.' If the hem is a work of such power and beauty, how much more the garment itself. If the garment is a work of such creativity and love, how much more the mind and heart of its Maker.

Anglican Restraint in the Presence of Scripture

God is mystery. And whatever reveals God must necessarily partake in some way of that mystery. If your theology or your piety or your reading of Scripture makes God entirely plain for you, that is good evidence that you need conversion. Only a faith that has room for surprise, only a theological structure that can be shaken by the Spirit without collapsing, is capable of perceiving God. This, I think, is the presupposition that grounds our tradition's approach to Scripture.

Anglicanism, in its understanding of the Bible, has been marked by this reserve or restraint, by a sense that one can never have it all, never reduce the Bible to a transparent system, never translate all that it has to say into some other more consistent or prosaic terms.

From the sixteenth century onward, we have had a complex relationship with the Continental Reformation. We welcomed its leadership in using the Bible as a means of conversion, as a way to return the fundamental insights of the faith to centre place in our common life. At the same

27

time, we resisted the tendency of some Lutherans to reduce everything to Paul or even to a particular Pauline doctrine; and we resisted the tendency of some Reformed leaders to treat Scripture as if it contained, in a somewhat oblique form, a detailed account of Christian life and belief and even of church polity.

From the Articles of Religion and Richard Hooker onward, we have maintained this reserve or restraint in what we say of Scripture. By 'reserve or restraint', however, I don't mean diffidence. Oh, we may have our share of that, too. I fear that my own guild of biblical scholars has been at least partly responsible for the current version of it. After listening to our academic battles, a good many Christians of all traditions have given up the hope of ever knowing what the Bible really means. Some of them, as a result, have given up reading it seriously. It is time for some serious taking of stock on that subject, but that is for another context.

What I mean by 'reserve or restraint' is not a matter of inadequate knowledge or of being afraid to speak up. At its best, it is a matter, rather, of an appropriation of the Bible rich enough and deep enough to make us aware of its complexities. I do not mean by that that we know all the scholarship. As far as I can tell, not even the scholars can know all the scholarship any more. I mean rather that we know and accept the complexity of the Bible itself, which cannot be reduced to a succinct theological unity.

We acquire this knowledge of Scripture not primarily in the classroom or the study, but in the context of prayer. I'm talking about the peculiarly Anglican way of reading, marking, learning and inwardly digesting Scripture within the basic context of the community at prayer. This practice may seem relatively unstructured and chaotic. And it is. But it has profound consequences. It suggests a centre for our reading, but declines to resolve the details. It creates a context of prayer. It assigns masses of Scripture to be read in it. And then it stands back to see what we make of it.

This practice includes both the Eucharist and the Daily Office. Both, of course, embody the worship of the community – the Daily Office as much as the Eucharist, even though it may often be read privately. But each works in a different way and provides a different context and scope for the readings. Both together have shaped our Anglican tradition of understanding the Bible. Each has contributed something of its own.

The Prayer of the Church and the Reading of Scripture

To begin with, what is common to Eucharist and Office in this regard? In both, Scripture is read in the context of worship. Anglicans have a long history of biblical study. We have never suggested that prayer is the *only* context for reading and absorbing Scripture. Still, this is our principal, our normative, context for reading it; and this makes a distinct difference to the process of reading. When one is at prayer, one is engaged in an interchange with God regarding those things that are of greatest importance in one's life. I don't mean the most solemn things, but rather the most revelatory ones. We give thanks and we complain. We plead, we resist and we surrender. We rejoice and we mourn. Thanks to our use of the Psalms, we learn pretty early on that we are not only permitted but expected to say what is on our mind. Equally, we are expected to listen. We expect to hear from God, through Scripture as well as through other mediums. We expect response, though it will not always take the form of an 'answer' in the narrow sense. We expect to engage in conversation with someone when we deal with Scripture.

All this the Eucharist and the Daily Office share. They assume that the reading and interpretation of Scripture form a part of the ongoing conversation between the worshipping community and God. That is very different from defining their context primarily in terms of the theologian's study. Both the method of interpretation and the expected result will be significantly different. More narrowly theological approaches may arise out of prayer, of course, and even help clarify prayer and move it toward greater profundity. I am not trying to separate the two from each other absolutely. A theology that is not rooted in prayer is likely to be arid. A prayer that never reflects on God, the world and the self is likely to be thoughtless and self-indulgent.

29

Still, the two are different. One rather crude and broad-brush way of suggesting the difference might be this: the theologian is looking for third-person formulations of what God is like and how God works; the worshipper is seeking second-person expressions of who God is and what God is saying to us. Where the theologian asks, 'Who is God?' and 'What does God say and do in the world?' the worshipper, says, 'Who are you?' and 'What are you saying or doing to me and to us?'

Ideally, the work of prayer and the work of theological reflection come together and influence each other. Yet, they remain different. They pull in different directions. Theology is a reflective genre, framed more in terms of understanding than of communion. Prayer, at its best, is the actual enjoyment of communion – with God and with the people of faith – an experience that challenges and transforms, converts and inspires and sends us onward to live in new ways, different, more honest, more just, more trusting, more loving. The two, when working well, lead back and forth, reflection to engagement, engagement to reflection. Indeed, in our muddled human way, we can barely tell which we're doing much of the time. Still, engagement is typically less tidy than reflection, reflection typically less immediate than engagement. As we shift from one mode to the other, we change a bit and our reading – of the Bible, of God, of ourselves, of the world around us – shifts, too.

Theology, alas, does not always remain in conversation with God. It can meander off on its own, become an idol in its own right, and set itself up as a replacement for God in this world. This is part of why the Church has to suffer the upheaval of reform from one age to the next. No sooner do we have the formularies resolved to our satisfaction than it turns out the whole process has been a distraction from something far more important. No matter how good the formularies are, the Spirit is always up to something else well before the last 'i' has been dotted and the last 't' crossed. Prayer, too, shows the same capacity for idolatry when we begin to prize the formulae of rites and ceremonies more highly than the conversation and communion with God they were intended to facilitate. Worship can go stale or, worse yet, become its own end.

But, at best or worse, our tradition invites us to incorporate the Bible first and foremost as an aspect of direct conversation with God rather than of theological reflection. The first step is not to think about it abstractly or incorporate it into ideas. The first step is to talk with God in, with and through the Bible.

The Eucharist Holds the Centre

In comparison with the Office, the Eucharist provides a good deal of guidance to the process. The Eucharist assumes a sermon.[3] The language of the preacher is related to that of the theologian. The preacher talks *about* God. And yet, a sermon is unpersuasive unless it captures some of the direct, engaged, unfinished quality of our ongoing conversation with God. A true sermon is not just a speech, much less an abstract treatise. It is a proclamation of God's Good News, a renewal of the surprise of grace, a reinvigoration of the possibility of hope. It can serve this purpose only when we, the worshippers, hear in it something of our own unfinished conversation with God. Then alone we can hope to hear how God is responding to us and engaging us. Like Jesus' parables, the sermon allows us to hear and see ourselves in a new light. It prompts not simply reflection but new vision and, therefore, change and renewal and movement toward communion.

The Eucharist structures and guides our reading of Scripture not only through the sermon but through the sacramental rite itself. The Eucharistic prayer brings us to the figure of Jesus and to the Cross and Resurrection as the centre of the whole conversation. It brings us to communion with Jesus and with one another in the sacrament of his Body and Blood. It does not try to include everything in the biblical story or in Christian faith. It establishes a centre for faith, which serves then as the interpretive touchstone of the rest. The Eucharist forms our faith, our prayer as Christians by giving it focus. But this means loss as well as gain. The process of giving form, after all, inevitably involves selection and deletion.

Not surprisingly, then, the eucharistic lectionary is relatively restricted. This was obvious in the old annual cycle, but it is still true in the contemporary multi-year lectionaries. In fact, it is a reality so familiar and necessary that we hardly notice it. I'm aware, for example, that American Episcopalians know quite a lot of Scripture, and yet they are often convinced that they're ignorant of it. They feel ignorant partly because they know the material aurally rather than visually and don't know where to find it in the pages of the Bible itself – this in a culture that has traditionally prized the citing of chapter and verse. But they also feel ignorant because the average Episcopalian's knowledge of Scripture is focused on the relatively small corpus of lessons read at the Eucharist. These are, for the most part, so central to Christian faith as to be beyond controversy; and, in the American context, with its strong element of Reformed Christianity, it has often been the knowledge of controversial texts that is prized.[4]

There is quite a lot of material in Scripture that we simply do not read at the Eucharist. I do not believe our tradition of eucharistic lections has ever included 'And Samuel hewed Agag in pieces before the Lord in Gilgal.'[5] Nor should it. What would it contribute in the eucharistic context? We do not need to read, either, about the Levite's concubine who was violated and left for dead at Gibeah or the massacre of the men of Benjamin that followed or the permission given the survivors to get themselves brides by means of rape.[6] Imagine having to explain any of that in a sermon – and trying to do it in such a way that it would no longer be a barrier to people's gathering at the eucharistic table.

Unfortunately, we do still read some things we should not have to. In the American church, at least, we still read the author to Ephesians admonishing women to obey their husbands, even though it may leave half or more of the congregation angry and alienated through the rest of the service. Or we read the passage from Romans 1 that is commonly understood as forbidding all same-sex sexual acts even though a good many of our congregations have a significant gay and lesbian presence. (I happen, myself, to believe that the usual interpretation is erroneous. But it takes a while to explain my reasons, and I cannot say I like trying to do it in a sermon.) With either of these passages, you can preach all you like about first-century social and cultural circumstances being different from ours, but it does little to remove the offence. The preacher who can keep such passages from being stumbling blocks has done well; to make them way stations along the path to communion with God and with one another seems almost impossible.

What makes such passages problematic in the Eucharist? It is not just that they are unpopular with some of us. The problem is that they drive some of us, some of the people the Spirit has brought into the church, away from God. Consciously or not, we expect the Eucharist to be relatively transparent to our conversation with God. We accept the formation it gives us. We are immersed in it. We are not on guard. And so we don't deal well in the eucharistic context with Scripture readings that have to be explained or even explained away.

I am not suggesting, of course, that the eucharistic readings can or should be undemanding. They have to reflect the breadth and complexity of human life and therefore the breadth and complexity of Christian faith. They need to deal with death as well as life, sin as well as redemption. Our faith is not easy or escapist, and there is no value in over-simplifying. But these texts do not have this kind of value. We have, to be sure, some co-religionists who consider the subordination of women and the rejection of gay and lesbian people to be core tenets of Christian faith. I am completely unable to understand how these can rank with the Trinity, the Creation, the Incarnation, the Cross and Resurrection, and the Giving of the Spirit. They are not of the same order of magnitude.

No matter what our differences about such issues, the eucharistic readings should not be used to marginalise groups within the community of the faithful. They should not be used to drive away those God has brought near – a recurring temptation of the Church ever since the first-century controversy over the admission of uncircumcised Gentile males. Compare an example that I think we are clearer about today. In all likelihood, we would not even suggest reading the Curse of Canaan at the Eucharist because of its history of being used to justify the oppression of people of colour. Whatever it may have meant in its own time and place, it is simply not acceptable at a Eucharist in our time. All eucharistic lections need to pass the test of whether they cooperate with the overall work of prayer and communion in the eucharistic rite.

The eucharistic lections, then, work only so long as they deal with matters of central value and importance. The Eucharist focuses our faith. The eucharistic lections need to serve that purpose, too; otherwise, they are working against their context. The Eucharist forms us by showing us and immersing us in the core of our conversation with God. This elevates it, and it also limits it. The Eucharist is not the context for reading the whole Bible.

The Daily Office: A Gift of Language

The Daily Office and its lectionary have had a very different role for Anglicans. The Office is not trying to identify the central thread of the Bible or of Christian faith. It creates, rather, a broad interaction with God in prayer and Scripture in a way that does relatively little to prescribe the details of that interaction. It supplies only the context of prayer in the environment of a Christian community. Indeed, Scripture and prayer merge with each other here in the use of Psalms and canticles. We read Scripture as broadly as we can manage, even if much of the time we find ourselves not simply absorbing it or looking through it to behold God, but wrestling with it. The Bible, it turns out, isn't always easy or helpful or transparent – at least not in any obvious way.

I do not mean that Anglicans, as a rule, read every last word of Scripture in the Daily Offices. The first Book of Common Prayer, for example, omitted extensive portions of Leviticus and Numbers, dealing with such topics as the liturgy of the Tabernacle and the purity code; and it excluded almost all of the Revelation of John. The current Office lectionary of the Episcopal Church includes the Revelation of John, but omits other things – for example, the gruesome story of the murder of the Levite's concubine that I mentioned earlier. Indeed, it displays a certain anxiety about violence in general and sometimes makes a curious hash of biblical narratives in an effort to avoid the more egregious verses.

34

Even given such omissions, however, our Office lectionaries are distinguished by extraordinary breadth. They include readings that are not conventionally edifying. They include a great deal that is secondary, from the eucharistic perspective, to Christian faith. What would be a fault in the eucharistic lectionary is a virtue in that of the Office, where the point is a broad encounter with the Bible without prescribing too closely what one is going to make of these readings. Indeed, if we pray the Office for any length of time, we must be prepared to meet things in Scripture that offend us, or seem irrelevant to Christian life today, or even threaten to put us to sleep.

At first glance, one might wonder why we would bother. I believe that some liturgists, in fact, find our Office an ungainly hybrid, overloaded with Scripture and unsuited to a worshipping community. Why? Because too much of the Scripture read in it is unedifying. Well, yes. There are problems with the Anglican version of the Office in a modern, industrial or post-industrial, mobile world. It was created, after all, for a world that was agrarian and much more settled. But whatever you think of the Office today, there can be little doubt of its influence in shaping Anglicanism over the last 450 years, for most of which it was actually the more common form of worship.

Those centuries of praying the Office have had several significant effects on our way of approaching and interpreting Scripture. One thing the Office has done is to create an allusive language compounded of Scripture and prayer – language with a power that freshly-minted language cannot always command. It is impossible to read our greatest poets, from George Herbert on, with full comprehension and enjoyment if you do not know both the Bible and the Prayer Book. And, if you do, you gain not merely increased comprehension of the poet's thinking but enhanced appreciation of the poetry's emotional power. Recognising an allusion to, say, the Song of Songs (not normally a part of eucharistic lectionaries, I believe) can deepen and broaden a poem in ways that defy ready explanation.

A favorite example of mine is a short and uncharacteristically hopeful poem by Henry Vaughan called *The Revival*:

Unfold, unfold! Take in his light,
Who makes thy cares more short than night.
The joys, which with his *Day-star* rise,
He deals to all but drowsy eyes:
And what the men of this world miss,
Some *drops* and *dews* of future bliss.
  Hark! how his *winds* have changed their *note*,
And with warm *whispers* call thee out.
The *frosts* are past, the *storms* are gone:
And backward *life* at last comes on.
The lofty *groves* in express joys
Reply unto the *turtle's* voice,
And here in *dust* and *dirt*, O here
The *lilies* of his love appear!

The poem begins with imagery of dawn and awakening, but then shifts to the image of a delayed spring, which finally arrives only after a long and stormy winter. When Vaughan refers to the voice of the turtle (or turtledove), he is carrying you back to the Song of Songs and its lovers' dialogue, which has also long been understood as the dialogue of the believer and God. At last, the unexpected appearance of the lilies of God's love, also from the Song of Songs, in the dust and dirt of our daily existence carries with it the revelatory power of the Incarnation itself. God's love is made fresh in the seemingly inappropriate context of the here and now.

If this gift of allusive language were the only thing the Daily Office had given Anglicanism, it would be gift enough. But there is more.

The Daily Office: A Gift of Seeing Scripture in Terms of Larger Wholes

A second gift we have received from our tradition of reading through Scripture in the Office is that it pushes us to read Scripture as a larger whole. Paradoxically, that is precisely because the individual snippets, day by day, make very little sense by themselves. They need, for starters, the context of the lections that precede and follow them. This is precisely what makes the communal observance of the

Office difficult in a highly mobile society, where attendance is usually sporadic and the worshipper loses the thread of continuity. If we want to read or hear the Office lessons on a regular basis, we have to locate or construct a continuity in which they can have meaning, whether it is a narrative continuity or a continuity of thought or a continuity of genre so that one recognises an oracle or a parable or a proverb for what it is.

The discontinuity that separates the lessons of one day from those that precede and follow compels the alert worshipper to exercise the skills of an attentive reader or listener. One begins distinguishing voices, for example, with their characteristic themes and tones. One notices a difference between what an Isaiah can say and what a Paul can say. One begins to sense the importance of the differing circumstances that make each voice possible and meaningful. We are willy-nilly introduced to a conversation that was already old before the time of Jesus. We are plunged into the middle of it to find out what it is about. The Eucharist gives you some clues. The Office is very sparing with them.

Even as the lessons at the Daily Office become a part of our conversation with God, we discover that they also belong to a conversation among human beings – human beings that did not always speak in the same way or agree with one another. To read Scripture in this way is a kind of introduction to the Communion of Saints, which turns out to be a rather rowdy family, united not by theological consensus so much as by a shared concern about human life in the presence of God. The biblical writers are looking for ways in which human life can make sense. They find the possibility of that, the hope of that, only by bringing God into the matter. But that does not mean that they always come up with the same answers.

After all, the exact same answers will not apply equally well in every possible human context. What made sense of human life with God in tribal, pre-monarchic Israel is not the same as what made sense of it in the reign of David or Solomon or under Assyrian or Babylonian domination. What made sense of it when the community of faith was a distinct, independent national group is not the same as what made sense of it for a small Jewish sect increasingly composed of Gentiles. Part of what we learn from the relatively indiscriminate reading of Scripture in the Office is that we must take circumstances seriously, that we must read with incarnational presuppositions. In the process, we can expect to hear a variety of voices far more diverse than many Christian traditions have supposed.

The Daily Office: A Gift of Reserve

The supreme gift the Office has given us is the all-important element of reserve that I mentioned earlier in this address. It trains us in this by presenting us with materials that seem utterly impossible to relate to one another. For example, the American lectionary, every other year, places readings from the Revelation of John alongside readings from Ecclesiasticus (or the Wisdom of Jesus ben Sira). I always find it a mind-bending experience. Here you have, on the one hand, readings that urge you to think of this world as a place of terrible but transient suffering, soon to be swept away and, on the other, readings that assume that this world will always go on more or less as it is and that what you really need is some good advice about honourable behaviour in polite society. There is truth, for better or worse, in each.

Another example arose for me this summer as I was beginning to think about this address. For a time, we were reading the beginning of Joshua alongside the end of Romans and the end of the Gospel of Matthew. What a bewildering experience! Joshua (obeying, we are told, the will of God) is taking possession of the Promised Land, committing genocide on its previous inhabitants, and trying to create a pure Israel worthy to inhabit the land. In the same narrative, we read about Rahab the prostitute, who betrays her city and her fellow citizens, and is rewarded for this deed by being saved from the slaughter, along with her family, and being married into the tribe of Judah. In an age of Rwanda and Kosovo, we recognise her.

Meanwhile, in the Gospel of Matthew, there is another betrayal. Judas betrays Jesus to the religious authorities. (But wait! This is the same Jesus who was, according to the beginning of Matthew's gospel, a descendant of the prostitute Rahab.) In this case, the betrayal is a sin, not a virtue; and God's agent Jesus – another Joshua, though the name is now in Greek form – suffers death rather than inflicting it. In fact, Jesus rebukes the disciple who draws a weapon, saying that those who take the sword will die by the sword and insisting that he himself has forsworn the aid of the legions of angels that are his by right.

Just to complicate matters a bit further, while we read of Joshua's bloody exploits and of the betrayal and death of Jesus, we also have Paul telling us that every human government has God's authority behind it (Rom. 13). One wonders if Paul really meant to include the city government of ancient Jericho or the court of Pontius Pilate. Christians, he says, are to obey the government – end of discussion. Within the Christian community, we are to owe no one anything except to love one another and, at all costs, to avoid judging one other.[7] How are we to understand Paul's God in relation to Joshua's? We have a strong commitment to reading the Bible as speaking of a single God. But what is one to make of reading all these passages alongside each other?

There is, I think, no simple and direct way to put all of this together. That is not to say that the job cannot be attempted. One possibility would be to invoke a dispensationalist methodology and say that God commanded slaughter in one era, but rejected it in another. One might get similar results from a developmental model. And perhaps we could suggest that Paul was speaking only to local concerns at Rome and not meaning to establish permanent rules about passivity in the face of tyranny or about generosity in the inner life of the Church. (How will we manage if we must really give up judging one another?) Yes, there are ways to force these texts into some common framework. But the Daily Office won't do the job for you any more than the Bible itself will. It will confront you with these seemingly incompatible texts and leave it up to you.

Worse yet, it will confront you with them in the context of prayer. How does one pray in the aftermath of Jericho and the other great genocides of history? How, in particular, does one pray to the God that the author of Joshua claims ordered that particular genocide? And how does one relate all that to Jesus, the descendant of the Canaanite Rahab who gained the lives of her family by betraying the rest of her people – a woman, incidentally, who would be despised by most Christians today for her profession? And how is it that Paul, who knows such a lot of Scripture, can hold up a standard of behaviour so radically different from that of Joshua?

I think there is little hope of *praying* in the context of these readings unless you are willing to accept that you still do not know all about God. I do not mean by that adopting a carelessly agnostic position. As Christians, we find the centre of our interpretation of God and of Scripture in the figure of Jesus. That is implicit in the Daily Office because it is explicit in the Eucharist. The image of the God who submits to violence, not the God who commands it, is our touchstone. We can begin our unravelling of the problems there. Joshua's act of genocide is not an option for us.

We have a centre, then. But we do not have the means to make it all neat, clean and rational. We are reminded again of the limitations on our grasp of God. We cannot merely drop the family stories, however painful they may be. Would there have been a Jesus without Israel? And would there have been an Israel without Joshua? We cannot extricate ourselves from the messiness of our history – the history, at any rate, that we claim for ourselves – by reading only the easier, more edifying bits, the passages that are more likely to get read at the Eucharist. We are talking with a God whose lilies appear in our mud.

I am not trying to justify Joshua. I do not know exactly how to judge one whose world was so radically different from my own. I can and will condemn the genocide – and, still more, the later genocides that Christians have justified by reference to the conquest of Canaan. But I do have to wonder what it meant for God to claim a people at the end of the second millennium BCE, in a place marked, it seems, by social collapse and tyranny and injustice. How could God speak into that situation a word that could be heard at all? How did Joshua's people know themselves claimed? Or how did they overcome their hatred of the Canaanites in order to incorporate Rahab and her kin? How are Jesus and Paul related to a history of violence that is, after all, almost universal among human beings? And how am I related to it?

I do not have final answers to these questions. In fact, I abjure final answers. This is the kind of reserve or restraint I spoke of earlier. I know where the centre of my faith is. It lies with the Jesus who died rather than kill. But I do not know how it will all work out, in my own life or the life of the world. What is more, I feel certain that anyone who does claim to know it all is deluded. The Bible is not a book of blueprints for church life, nor an ingeniously disguised treatise on systematic theology. It is a long, complicated, messy, sometimes wrong-headed family discussion with and about God. We are privileged to overhear it and to continue it. We are not authorised to clean it all up and make it presentable for our own time.

This makes the Bible less than some of our co-religionists would have it be; it cannot tell us nearly as much as they would like. It makes it less absolute, less readily intelligible, less self-consistent. But it also makes the Bible more. It makes it more a record of genuine exchange between God and humanity, a humanity still struggling along the way that God invites us and enables us to follow, the path of God's love, which is as difficult for Anglicans as for others.

An Anglican Way

If Anglicans have an advantage, it is not that we are holier, but that we have learned to sense the limits of what we can know. I think it is, above all, our peculiar practice of the Daily Office that has taught us this. It could not do so without our parallel practice of the Eucharist, forming us in the central affirmations of our faith. Still, it is the Daily Office through which we have received the gift of reserve and restraint – the gift to hold back from sweeping and universal claims to the knowledge of God's will. Through the Daily Office, God has given us a gift of living with ambiguity and uncertainty. Through the Daily Office, we have learned to read the Scriptures as part of an ongoing

41

conversation with God and with God's people of every age.

Of course, we have trouble hanging onto that. Anglicans are as prone to idolatry as anybody. Another way of saying that is that we are as uncomfortable with ambiguity and uncertainty as anybody. We try out this idol and that. Some of us think God only recognises the prayers of one particular edition of the Book of Common Prayer. Some of us think God only works through male priests ordained in a certain way. Some of us think God only speaks through their particular theology. What Jesus and the Spirit want us to do is to cast down the idols and stand in the presence of God undefended by them.

I do not mean by that that we should throw away the Prayer Book or the bishops or the Bible itself. I mean that we should throw away the unorthodox and unfaithful expectation that they can ever *contain* God, that God can ever be completely open to our understanding. The life of God is a mystery – a life-giving, loving mystery. The Trinity's love is generative not only of its own life, but of the life of all the worlds that ever have been and ever will be. This Trinity comes, again and again, in search of the creatures it has made and loved and seeking our love in return. The story of that search is the family story of the Communion of Saints. It is complicated by the mystery of God's love and by our own difficulty in grasping or giving voice to it.

That is not easy to understand. It will never be easy to understand. The Church, the worship of the Church, and the Bible in the context of that worship all help bring us into a conversation. At its best, the conversation will give rise to flashes of understanding – the flashes we need in order to draw more closely into communion with God and with all those whom God loves. That is enough. That's more than enough. And it's a good thing, for it is all we have got.

It is a mistake to regard the Bible as a book of answers, as some of our co-religionists have done. It is a book of unfinished mystery, a book of many voices, a book of encounter, a book that serves God's purpose in loving us and drawing us together into God's embrace. It is a great help to have the Eucharist and its lectionary identifying a thread to follow. It's also vital to have the Office exposing us to the larger and richer array of the whole. From the combination of the two, comes a sense of engagement that is also reserve – not a reserve arising from ignorance and inexperience, but a reserve arising from knowing the Bible's breadth and complexity and being deeply involved with one who is always doing something new.

The Bible is not a book that answers all questions. It is a book that keeps inspiring new questions, new insights, new conversion and change of heart in us. If, in the process, it brings us to touch just the hem of God's garment, what a moment of glory and delight! To insist on more would be to miss the point.

Notes

1 Wilfrid Cantwell Smith has remarked on the propensity of Anglicanism to read Scripture 'through' the Book of Common Prayer in *What Is Scripture? A Comparative Approach* (Minneapolis: Fortress Press, 1993), p. 205. I think one could actually say that we approach Scripture primarily through the experience of prayer as the BCP structures it.
2 Mark 5; Matt. 9; Luke 8.
3 The classic rubrical pattern is to specify preaching only at the Eucharist.
4 This tendency was also strong in seventeenth century England. I think it provided the motivation for George Herbert's admonition that the preacher should choose 'texts of Devotion, not Controversy, moving and ravishing texts, whereof the Scriptures are full' (*The Country Parson*, ch. vii).
5 1 Sam. 15:33.
6 Judg. 19–21.
7 Rom. 13:8–10; 14:10–13.

4 The Sermon*

Rowan Williams

Preaching has become an anodyne word, often sadly reflecting an anodyne reality. It is one of those words, rather like 'church', whose meaning we think we know – whereas, when it was first used in the first Christian century, it was not at all so clear what it meant. Or rather, in the world of the first century of our era, it *was* clear what it meant, in general usage, and therefore extremely unclear what it meant in the Christian context. People knew what a *kerux* was: a herald, an announcer of Royal proclamations and decrees.

When King Nebuchadnezzar decreed that all those who heard the music of the various instruments described in the book of Daniel should fall down and worship his image, the herald, the *kerux*, the preacher, was telling you something that you really needed to know – as Shadrach, Meshach and Abednego duly found out. The Coverdale translation of Psalm 68:11, referring to 'the company of the preachers' is again about those who run around telling you what you need to know; most specifically, the news you need to know from official sources: news that will make a difference; news of events, victories or defeats; news of decrees from authority; news of promises and demands being made; all sorts of things. But above all, it is the telling of news which makes a difference.

When St Paul reflects on what it is to proclaim, to be a herald for the events of Jesus' life and death and resurrection he seems often to be aware of the many ironies around the use of the word. There is irony enough in being a royal herald charged with the news of an execution, the execution

*© Rowan Williams 2000

44

of the king. The irony is heaped higher when to be a royal herald, charged with this news, is also to be the prisoner dragged at the tail end of the official procession (1 Cor. 4:9): God has made us apostles, who are 'the off-scouring of all things'. Paul knows that the use of this apparently clear word, *Kerux*, in the Christian context is at least as confusing as using the word *ekklesia*, or citizens' assembly, for that bizarre assortment of odds and ends who meet in attic rooms in Corinth to break bread.

So, if we want to rescue preaching from the anodyne meaning with which so often we find ourselves endowing the word, we need to focus, first and foremost, on preaching as the annunciation of a change. Something is different. Change is possible: Jesus Christ makes it so, and the Bible records that change. And it is within all that change recorded in Scripture that the preacher, the proclaimer, works. Change is possible because Christ makes it so; and that is why preaching is not the same as teaching.

That is why, when St Paul talks about preaching and proclamation in his letters, he is thinking of something that has some overlap with, but yet is significantly different from the practice of expounding Scripture in the synagogue setting. Exposition may well enter in, but it is not actually the very heart of what Paul means by proclamation. When you use the Scriptures in proclamation, you use them not simply as a text on which to reflect in general or as a set of problems needing elucidation. You use them as part of this complex process of saying that a change has occurred. You think through the changes, the transformations in the Scriptures, as you proclaim, because what you are proclaiming is an event of transformation.

This is why the act of preaching has a sacramental quality, in the sense that and to the extent that it is about transformation. The words of proclamation are words that both enact and enable change, the kind of change that is made possible by the life and death and resurrection of Jesus Christ. It is in this sense that all preaching is, as a certain Christian tradition would say, preaching for conversion. Every time an act of proclamation occurs, it both witnesses to and enacts a certain kind of change. A transformation has occurred; but now, what difference does it make to me and to you? Playing on the venerable verbal confusion between conversion and conversation, it is a conversion which occurs in being drawn into the conversation between God and God's people, the conversation which is the heart of Scripture.

Having made the general point about proclamation and change, we need now to ask about the identity and purpose of the preacher, the one who proclaims. The person who proclaims all this has to be, herself or himself, a person who believes that change is possible. This may sound rather obvious, but perhaps it isn't; and perhaps there is too much preaching or proclamation which in fact starts from the assumption not only that change is impossible, but that, even if it were possible, it would be highly undesirable.

More seriously, if the passion and integrity of one's preaching does not rest on, or arise from (and this will sound very evangelical) a personal conviction that conversion is possible, one might as well shut up. When I preach, what I ought to be doing is witnessing to conversion in myself, and in others. The only reason I have any authority to speak as a preacher, is because of the sense in the Church at large, which I have accepted and heard, and made my own, that change is possible; that transformation has occurred, is occurring and will occur. And therefore I not only preach for conversion, I preach *from* conversion.

This needs a bit of nuancing. One way in which preaching has too often been envisaged is as a process of decanting achieved or acquired understanding and wisdom from the vast resources in the pulpit into the rather small pot sitting in front. But if I understand correctly what my own conversion is actually about, then I shall know, of course, that my attempt to proclaim the Word is and can only be part of the continuing process of my own transformation.

My favourite story of John Wesley, one which will be known to many of you, is his encounter with Peter Böhler, a Moravian, on the voyage back from Georgia in 1738 (after Wesley had had what we would call a nervous breakdown in Georgia, after a miserable love affair, the disastrous, public humiliations attendant upon it, and a general feeling that he had made a total mess of his first attempt at evan-

46

gelism; an experience not a million miles away from that of many of us, I guess). How was he going to go back as a cleric of the established Church and preach? Böhler famously said to him, 'Preach faith until you have it.' In other words, your ability and your authority to preach rests in significant measure upon your own awareness of your need. You preach not only out of your conversion, but out of your hunger.

In that sense it is very like the sacraments overall. Sacraments bear witness to decisive change, and yet they do not say that the story is over, that the transformation has occurred once and for all, and that is it. Baptism has to be renewed and re-appropriated. The Eucharist is celebrated again and again and again, daily, weekly. Transformation continues because the material on which the transforming power of God works is us, and we are often, as I hinted earlier, deeply resistant to the idea that transformation is possible or desirable. Preaching rests on the same set of assumptions as regular sacramental practice – that what I witness to, in terms of my conversion or hoped for conversion, is always incomplete. The more deeply I am converted, the more hungry I become, the more deeply I realise my unconversion. I preach into and out of that situation. It's a cliché, I suppose, but like many clichés not without truth, that the best sermons are the ones you preach to yourself. And at one level you are, I think, constantly preaching to yourself: preaching faith until you have it. Which is to say that preaching, the proclamation of the good news of Jesus Christ, is always necessarily an action undertaken in *hope*. When the preacher gets up into the pulpit, that is a sign of hope. The habitual sinking of the heart which may accompany that moment on the part of the congregation is just one of those unfortunate cultural and human facts which we have to live with – but also an index of just how difficult it is to preach hope, and to make preaching an event of hope. When Bonhoeffer compared preaching to the holding out of a large red apple to a hungry child, he was expressing something similar. We ought to feel that the hunger of the preacher is connecting with our own hunger, and the preacher just might know where there is food to be had. Again, it's a familiar saying that preaching is one hungry person telling another where there is food.

I preach in hope. I preach therefore in an awareness of what it is that *I* need to hear, and what it is that *I* am hungry to hear. So, thinking about preaching involves a complex and interesting process of looking at myself and my faith, and quarrying, you might say, for what it is that you and I *both* need. Here is where things can get difficult. I have heard sermons, and so have you, that have been a good deal about the preacher's need, and which have not always necessarily connected with anybody else's; just as I have heard sermons, and so have you, which may attempt to meet a congregation's need but do not appear to come out of any sense of need on the preacher's part. It's a knife-edge, isn't it? I am thinking in the latter case of the kind of sermon which presses the right buttons, which uses the right slogans, which apparently connects with what people are most eager to hear – eager, but not necessarily hungry. And so at the end of the sermon you may say that that was precisely what matched the expectations and the surface desires of the congregation; but that somehow it did not come out of the hunger of the preacher for discovery – just as the preacher who is exploring desperately his or her own need and uncertainty in the pulpit may be wrapped up in a cocoon protecting them not only from the need of the congregation, but the reality of the world.

Quarrying for what it is that you and I both need is by no means a simple job. The question of how what I need to say might meet your hunger will only be seriously answered when I begin to understand how my hunger and yours connect. And that's why, of course, good preaching always entails, and arises out of good listening. This is also why it is so difficult for bishops to preach good sermons, because we go from place to place and congregation to congregation, and our opportunities for listening are limited, and we have to find other opportunities for trying to learn and to be attentive even to *begin* to be audible when we preach. The preaching that matters is precisely the preaching that comes out of a steady and patient and deeply attentive listening to those whose needs you are speaking into.

Preaching then is the annunciation of a change, a challenge to see how that change changes you, the hearer, but
also changes me, the proclaimer. It is to do with the hunger
for change, the hunger for the kind of transformation that
will take me closer to the source of reality, and therefore
closer, strange as it may seem, to those I speak to. Bizarre,
isn't it, that preaching has become one of those words (and
all too often one of those realities) that accentuates the gap
between the speaker and those spoken to: 'six feet above
contradiction', 'don't preach at me' – these are expressions
which reflect a lack of anything you could call shared
hunger.

All this helps us to focus on a set of quite complicated
issues about what it is like to be 'personal' when you are
preaching. How are we to make sense of this? We read the
great sermons of the classical preachers of our tradition (all
the time, I'm sure . . .) and are likely to say, 'Oh but this
is very impersonal. These are disquisitions on matters of
theology and ethics, little lectures.' We cannot do it this
way these days. The expectation is that we be personal, as
I commented earlier when I wrote of the essential quality
in preaching as personal witness and conversion. Do I then
preach my story in the pulpit? 'Indeed I do', say lots of
people with gusto; you've heard them, too. Here is a
tension, which like many of the tensions with which we
live, does not go away in a hurry. When I was first ordained
(I am being 'personal' now, you will have noticed . . .), I
remember making a resolution which lasted about two
years into my ordination, that I would not use the first
person singular in the pulpit. It was a puritanical and
pharisaical resolution, but I think I could defend as real
enough the concern out of which it came. I felt (even at
that relatively tender age) that I had heard enough sermons
larded with the first person singular to last me a lifetime.
What I am doing when I am preaching is not simply saying,
'This is what the Lord has done for *my* soul.' It is saying,
'This is what the Lord has done for *us*'; and I know the Lord
has done this for us, because I speak from the perspective
of that us. When I listen to a sermon, I am not looking for
an individual set of experiences, but for the experience of
the Church, the experience of the community. And it is

49

possible so to describe what is going on because being personal, as you all know, is something different from being simply *individual*.

Nonetheless, we recognise that we now live in an age in which sincerity is habitually identified with a particular kind of rather forced intimacy. Sincerity means having what an earlier Christian generation would call the passions very near the surface. And reading Bill Countryman's words elsewhere in this volume about Anglican reserve may remind us that it was not always so. Again we tread a knife-edge. Impersonality, rigorous suspicion of emotion and all the rest of it have not served us well. I am just not sure, however, if we are being served very much better in a culture where sincerity means an attempt at instant transparency, because there is no such thing. Moreover, when I am speaking so directly from my experience in the pulpit that what you are focusing on is my experience, I am standing in your light. This point is hard to grasp sometimes, and yet crucial to the activity of preaching. Sincerity is not forced intimacy, and being personal is not being autobiographical. How each of us works that out when we attempt to proclaim, in the pulpit or elsewhere, is something we shall not answer in a hurry.

When it is doing its job, a sermon, you could say, is a kind of performing of the Gospel. When I think of other kinds of professional performance, what I expect of a good actor is certainly that he or she will be sincere, that is to say that their resources of mind and body are put whole-heartedly at the service of a pattern of words, of evoked feeling – hope, despair, desire – in such a way that the person speaking and acting becomes transparent to something greater than what they are. You can't do that without sincerity. But if the actor in the middle of Hamlet's famous soliloquy broke of to say, ' . . . and that reminds me of something which I feel very, very deeply, and need to share with you . . .', I would not regard that as a good performance of Hamlet: it would not be transparent to what was actually being performed.

When I preach, I hope to make my own the story of God's dealings with God's people. I hope and trust that I am struggling to bring to light a reality that has been in part internalised, yet remains utterly itself, not something domesticated into me. That process of making it my own is something very different from possessing or mastering the text so that it is drawn into my story. What happens, as with Hamlet, though in a rather different way, is that the text I make my own displaces quite a lot of the usual way I talk and think and act. Preaching, like acting, comes out of that displacement. That is why we come to speak of transparency.

Preaching is an invitation into a world not bounded by my understanding as an individual, or my experience as an individual. So if all this about transformation, witness and conversion is true, the challenge is that the preacher is finding out through that transformation and conversion that there is no closure of the whole truth about himself or herself. The enterprise still involves what the person has enjoyed, what the person has feared, believed and doubted, what the person has understood and not understood.

There are no general answers which can ultimately relieve us of that tension: it is just one of those things that ought to be there as a persistent worry for any preacher. It is just one of those God-given, glorious, creative, graceful worries that people trying to proclaim the Gospel ought to have. Let no one pretend that being a Christian, or proclaiming the Christian faith, is a release from worry! Though I'd better make it clear that I am distinguishing creative worry from the sheer, agonising individualised anxiety that so easily paralyses us. What I am alluding to are the creative worries that are prompted by those questions without which we would not grow and move. I mean those constant and constructive irritants which the hearing of the Gospel always generates in us. Good preaching, I think, has to arise out of such constructive worry. How am I transparent? How do I let what I am speaking of displace myself? How do I enact in the pulpit the change I am talking about? How does the medium become the message?

Earlier in the text I used the word invitation. Change is often frightening because it can come across to people not as invitation, but as demand: 'You *must* change.' Such a challenge is there in the proclamation of the Gospel and we must not pussyfoot around it. And yet of course, when

51

one reads the gospels, the extraordinary paradox and the power of the proclamation of the Kingdom from the mouth of Jesus is that it is both demand and invitation. The parables concerning the invitations to the royal feast are very, very strange. They are commands. If you disobey those commands terrible things happen to you. At the same time, they are also invitations to such joy and fulfilment and fellowship that you ought to understand that if you say no to them, more than just your happiness is at stake: you become less than yourself. How again you weld those together in such a way that the invitation does not become collusive, and the demand does not become oppressive, however . . . there's another knife-edge tread for a person trying to proclaim the Gospel. Yet invitation it is, and as Walter Brueggemann[1] repeatedly reminds us, invitation into a larger world, into a re-organised world. We become part of a world of speech and insight and imagery that is different from what we concoct for ourselves.

This is why, of course, proclamation is so rightly and properly enshrined at the heart of the Eucharist. If we are thinking about where transformation really occurs, the Eucharist tells us, shows us, enacts in us the change that Jesus Christ effects. We are there at the Eucharist so that we may be changed into his likeness, from glory to glory. We are there not to change certain things in the world, which we then adore from a distance. We are there so that the transubstantiation may occur *in us*. As George Herbert says in one of his poems on the Holy Communion, transubstantiation would make sense as a theory only if God were more interested in bread than in us. We dare not forget that the change in the bread is so that there will be a change in us. So the sermon, as a moment in the eucharistic transaction, is precisely bound up with the changes that are going on, and will go on, in us, in the whole business of our living in the Body of Christ, and most specifically in our receiving of the elements of the Holy Eucharist.

The sermon is the proclamation of good news because it is itself transformed and transforming speech. It is transformed speech because it does not just repeat what the world says, nor does it just repeat what the Bible says. It attempts to show, in its movement, in its direction and

52

imagery, what it is to be in a different world, another kingdom. It is the invitation to the Kingdom of God. Indeed, in the invitation itself, already the Kingdom has begun to come, the change has begun to occur.

It is here, I suppose, that differences again arise between interpreters and preachers as to the role of emotion in preaching. Emotion is one of the transforming forces in our lives, and we can sometimes therefore be misled to suppose that when we have an emotion a transformation is necessarily occurring. Preachers are divided between those who step back very firmly from it and others who say, 'But it's true, emotion is part of our transformation, and we have to deal with that part of our humanity as with other things.' Read the wonderful quote from Herbert used by Bill Countryman in his chapter about how preaching should address the passions, should move because of the need to experience Scripture as a source of delight.

But in apparent sharp contrast to Herbert's approach is that of the other great patriarch of our tradition, Richard Hooker, who seems to have rather disapproved of preaching that stirs up the passions. There is a wonderful description of Hooker preaching in the Temple Church, which gives a very vivid picture of the great man in the pulpit – his voice low and weak, his stature unimpressive, speaking almost without moving from the beginning of the sermon to the end. In other words, Hooker simply stood there reading these enormous discourses in a virtual monotone and almost inaudibly. Judith Maltby has said bluntly, 'Obviously, Hooker was a perfectly terrible preacher.'[2] And yet, my favourite among Hooker's sermons, one of the great tracts on perseverance ('The certainty and perpetuity of faith in the elect', preached in 1585), is in fact an immensely engaging and involving sermon, precisely about transformation. It dwells upon the glorious and the unmanageable possibilities of faith, and about how faith grows and sustains itself in the very midst of emotional darkness. It is one of the masterpieces of Anglican devotional writing. Hooker's delivery may have been deplorable by modern (or Elizabethan) standards, but what he wanted was to stir godly feeling as well as truthful thought.

Again and again we come back to the knife-edges of preaching, in a way which I suppose is inevitable if we are talking about transformation, because transformative activity is always something poised between two worlds; which is a dangerous place to be. The preacher inhabits what the sociologist would call a liminal place, a place where worlds overlap, languages and visions overlap. It is not a comfortable place to be and we need reminding of that. The person who is fluent and easy in the pulpit is someone to be suspected as much as the person who is unprepared and inarticulate. How our use of language demonstrates the right kind of difficulty with its subject matter is quite a challenge. Herbert speaks of how the preacher should from time to time turn towards the altar and apostrophise God, in what might, I suspect, be regarded as rather a manipulative gesture these days. Herbert might say, so he indicates in his advice to preachers: 'Lord, please make them understand what I am saying, because it is really important.' What Herbert is actually doing here is what he is doing in his poetry very often, by those unpredictable changes of direction and tone that he's so very good at. Frequently he is saying something like: 'I have come to the end. I do not know what to say any more. Methought I thought I heard one calling, "Child", and I replied "My Lord".' I think that is part of what he is trying to say when he reflects on preaching in *A Priest to the Temple:* that there are moments in our preaching when we really do come to the end of what we have to say; and how we express that, goodness only knows. In a less innocent age than Herbert's as regards apostrophising the Lord audibly in such circumstances, we are perhaps at a disadvantage.

We must not lose sight, nonetheless, of the fact that preaching is no more difficult than any other bit of Christian speaking. Doctor Johnson said, when someone was moaning about the hardships of the married state, 'Sir, marriage is not otherwise unhappy than as human life is unhappy.' By the same token, preaching is not otherwise difficult than as Christian talking in general is difficult. And Christian talking in general is difficult because all Christian talking in some sense boils over from conversion, transformation and the consequent awkwardness of living in two worlds. Preaching is an acute case of it because someone has been asked to stand before the assembly and articulate something of why it is so difficult to articulate about Christian things. It is almost as if we were saying to the Christian preacher, 'Just stand there and tell us why it is difficult to talk about God.'

And why is it difficult to talk about God? Because God is different, and the source of difference, and the source, the wellspring of change. It is difficult because when we draw near to God things change unpredictably. The bread and wine become the instruments of the light and life of Christ delivered into our hands and into our lives. It is difficult because Christian speech is about silence and the Word, about dying and rising. That is why it is the challenging role of the preacher, wrestling with that difficulty, to remind us why difficulty matters. Difficulty is central because change is difficult and difficult to understand. Transformation is not obvious. It is about becoming other. The preacher goes into the pulpit to proclaim that difficulty, that difference, proclaiming the events and the transactions that we really need to know about if we are not to be left locked up in a prison of our own imaginations and wills and feelings. Preaching is springing us from the trap of our egos. Which is why of course the pulpit is just the tip of the iceberg, a sign of that whole process of speaking and acting which attempts very inadequately to say what it is that has changed through that unspeakable transaction, transformation and difference that occurs through Jesus Christ.

Notes

1 *Finally Comes the Poet: Daring Speech for Proclamation, The Introduction* (Fortress Press, 1989).
2 In *The Pelican Record* (Vol. XL, Dec. 1999), the *alumni* magazine for Corpus Christi College, Oxford.

5 The Creed*

Averil Cameron

In some ways the Creed today seems to be the poor relation of the other elements of the Eucharist. It does not even have a proper name, 'creed' simply being a shorthand English version of the first Latin word *credo*. It has been called by many names, including 'symbol', or *regula* (rule of faith), or just 'the faith of Nicaea'. When the service has to be shortened, it is the Creed that is usually omitted. Many of us, including myself, feel awkward when reciting it, almost as if we were required to stand up and subscribe to the Thirty-Nine Articles, and few of us know much in detail about its history or how it came to be there.

I too fell into the trap in the past of thinking that the Creed was requiring us to state that we believed in the literal truth of all the propositions it seemed to contain. Despite a Church of England upbringing, an Oxford training in philosophy at a time when proof was thought to exist only when there was empirical evidence made me feel distinctly uncomfortable. Then there are the actual phrases used – 'Very God of Very God' (what does *that* mean?), or 'being of one substance with the Father' (what does 'substance' mean?). We say these words almost unconsciously and without thinking – until we ask ourselves what they mean. The fact that this *is* still a problem is obvious for example from the fuss that arose over David Jenkins' famous comments about the Virgin birth, and I strongly suspect that a very large number of people are simply confused about the Creed, what it is and why it is there.

We cannot duck it though. For instance, as R. P. C.

*© Averil Cameron 2000

Hanson pointed out, it is used as a given in ecumenical discussion.[1] The Creed is not a prayer. It was, historically, a serious attempt to state the essence of orthodox doctrine. But it is a pretty strange document. The same scholar refers to it as 'an eclectic composition of late Greek philosophy' and says (quite rightly I am sure) that 'the huge majority of those who repeat this creed regularly [in whatever translation] are completely unaware' of the circumstances in which it came into existence.

We cannot cope with it by pretending that it is just a set of rather high-sounding poetic expressions. The Creed is not poetry. It was meant as a rigorous statement of agreed doctrine – committee-speak, in a real sense. It has been identified as one of the four principles of Anglicanism, with the Old and New Testaments and the episcopacy. Or it has been described as our lowest common denominator. It was on the lips of Thomas Cranmer as he faced his burning. There has to be a way in which modern worshippers can make it their own.

What are some of the difficulties? First of all, even if it is couched as far as possible in biblical language, the Nicene, or 'Nicene–Constantinopolitan' Creed is not scriptural. Secondly, it did not come into being as such until the fourth century AD and it was not part of the eucharistic liturgy until quite a while after that. Thirdly, even though it is referred to as the Nicene Creed, that description is mistaken: it is not the Creed of Nicaea but a later and much enlarged version or variant of it. It may not even be the 'Nicene–Constantinopolitan Creed', in that the enlargement may not have been the work of the Council of Constantinople in 381. Fourthly, it is not a relatively simple statement of faith like the baptismal formula, but rather, a carefully worked out public document which belongs to a particular moment in time and a particular set of controversies which are not on the whole the controversies of our time. Finally, it preserves a cosmology and a typology of salvation which pose real problems today, and uses philosophical or figural phraseology which only makes sense in a certain context, such as 'begotten of his Father before all worlds', or 'God of God'.

I would like to start by asking about its *function* – not its function when it was composed (I shall come to that later), but its function now.

At its present place in the liturgy, the Creed comes after the readings and the homily. So the worshipper has been instructed, by listening to the word of God and perhaps by having it explained in the homily, or having received the proclamation, in Rowan Williams' formulation, and been transformed. By the recital of the Creed he expresses his belonging to the community of the Church. It may be helpful therefore to regard the Creed's language as *performative* – it is a proclamation of belonging, even of *wishing* to belong, on the part of everyone. We must get away from the notion that the Creed consists of propositional statements, statements of 'fact', and hang on to the idea that it expresses something about the relationship of the worshippers to the Church, to the Christian community as a whole. Saying things together is a badge of belonging.

How our Creed originated and how it is used today in the liturgical context are two separate issues. But we might want to remember that the eucharistic liturgy as we know it developed slowly. Our Creed did not enter it until at least the fifth century AD, and then only in a very *ad hoc* and unclear way. The Emperor Justin II ordered it to be included officially in the eucharistic liturgy only in AD 568, two hundred years after the enlarged version seems to have evolved. And this in itself is only an isolated scrap of information – we really cannot assume that the order was immediately followed everywhere. So our Creed was not in existence from time immemorial. It was not a feature of the eucharistic liturgy from the beginning. And although there were many credal statements, and, as it were, credal fragments, statements of belief, in earlier writers from apostolic times onwards, our Creed did not develop directly out of any of them.

Our Creed is a historical survival from a very particular period in the history of the Church. When I was in York Minster recently I found that the service card introduced the Creed by saying just this – that it represents how the faith was formulated and understood during the fourth century AD – and I thought how good that was as an explanation of what must seem pretty difficult to a newcomer, and also how well it put the matter for the average communicant.

There were certainly creeds – or statements of belief – before this Creed. The so-called 'declaratory creeds', short statements of belief, are generally associated with baptism, and we have pretty good fourth and fifth century evidence for this.[2] But creeds are not the same as the questions asked of a candidate for baptism, and anyway these are not our Creed; obviously there is a connection, but the early evidence for baptism is too complicated for us to be able to say that the Nicene Creed developed out of baptismal creeds. On the other hand statements of faith were also required for instruction ('catechesis'). But this does not mean that there was in existence an early fixed form from which our Creed developed. Many forms of credal statement can be found, and for different reasons. But the idea that there was from an early date a fixed formulary, at Rome or elsewhere, is hard to substantiate (let alone the idea that the Apostles' Creed was drawn up by the apostles). A better picture, it would seem, is of a multiplicity of local statements contributing in their different ways to a a new Creed agreed at Nicaea.

Why was it necessary to 'state the faith'? On the whole, neither pagans nor Jews did it. So why Christians? Part of the answer about 'statements of faith' might have to do with self-identity – the effort of early Christians to distinguish themselves from others – first of all pagans and Jews, but also from Gnostics, and Christians who were not regarded as mainstream. We see it already in the Acts of the Apostles. It is a main theme in the second-century writers like Irenaeus, Justin and Tertullian, and it continually gets up more steam. One of the main themes of Christian writers in the second and third centuries, and of course later, is to establish what is and is not orthodox, simply meaning 'correct'. And it is quite striking that some of the fullest credal statements in the early period, in Irenaeus and Tertullian, do in fact come from works written against heresy.[3] I would want to say that much as it would be appealing to be able to trace an unbroken line back to the apostles, 'the Church' did not spring fully formed at Pentecost. It had to be constructed, and its agreed beliefs

59

(note the word 'agreed') evolved painfully and, to use down-to-earth language, by a long process of what Hanson has called trial and error.[4] God did not make it easy.

How does this affect the modern worshipper and the saying of the Creed today? A young American scholar has drawn attention to what she calls 'the performance of orthodoxy'.[5] Settling what was orthodox was not just a matter of argument, factual or otherwise; it was a matter of practice, of persuasion, of staking a claim, of establishing your group as being right. This required not just debate, but other forms of persuasion as well: repetition, slogans, public affirmation, in fact in literary–critical language, performative utterance. In saying the Creed, the modern worshipper assents to the collective history and the current and future community of the Church as the bearer of orthodoxy. He or she may think he is describing his own beliefs, but actually he/she is associating himself as a member with the Christian group.

Our Creed does not place the modern emphasis on 'sincerity' or the personal. It is a complex text, arrived at in more than one stage and from varied sources. This may be the place to ask what the word 'catholic' means in the Creed's last paragraph. It does not mean Roman Catholic as opposed to Anglican. Nor does it mean Catholic as opposed to Protestant. In its fourth-century use, which the Creed preserves, it means 'the whole Church', that is, those who rightly claim to be orthodox. In a famous formulation from the fifth century 'catholic' belief is 'that which has been believed everywhere, always and by all'.[6] But that is a claim too, and a bold one. This last paragraph containing the reference to the catholic church was not part of the original Nicene version, though it preserves older credal traditions. It has as much of an axe to grind as the others. It too stakes a claim. (And so does the word 'apostolic': not everyone accepted this Creed but nobody would deny that his church was apostolic.)

It would be going too far to say that in large part formulating a statement of belief arose precisely out of trying to prove that someone else was wrong. Yet Robert Markus has written of what he calls the first phase of self-identification that the accent was 'on defining the hallmark of the true Christian church among its competitors, not on identifying true doctrine'.[7] Our Creed is far from being a straightforward attempt to formulate belief; it is a mixture of fragments recognisable in scriptural and other early sources, and phrases whose function is to exclude an alternative formulation, i.e. in part at least it is a piece of polemic. The trouble is that today we have mostly forgotten what the polemic is all about. It is also too long and too detailed for comfort – or perhaps for what is needed today – and as we saw it is quite often simply dropped.

There was a strong need for creeds in connection with baptism. But the Creed that was drawn up and signed by nearly all those present at the Council of Nicaea in AD 325 marked a very major new departure. We can see the signs of this already, in the equation of creeds with tests of orthodoxy – the Council of Arles in 314, also called by Constantine, referred to accepting a creed as the test of orthodoxy, and Arius and Alexander both drew up creeds to represent their own positions.[8] But the Council of Nicaea was different in scale, and in its degree of 'officialness', being called by the emperor to settle division once and for all. Its Creed was not a baptismal statement; it was a document drawn up by and for bishops, and signing it was made a test of their orthodoxy and accompanied by state sanctions: the few who refused were exiled by order of the emperor. The Council of Nicaea was not about liturgy and this was not a liturgical text even if it later came to be used as such; it was almost an official communiqué. The Emperor Constantine addressed and admonished the bishops who were present, and wrote to those who were not, informing them about it; he also sent them lavish presents.[9] But we don't know how the bishops were supposed to use the document. Furthermore, it did not contain the last paragraph of our Creed (the Holy Spirit was not the point, or rather the person, at issue at the Council), and was briefer and somewhat different in the detail. It ended with anathemas pronounced against those it implicitly condemned.

In a real sense the Creed of Nicaea *was* intended as an ecumenical document. Constantine knew that there were serious divisions and wanted them settled. He had not been successful in his attempts to reconcile the Donatists in North Africa, and he probably wanted the date of Easter to be settled as much as the relation of the Son to the Father. In any case he was not prepared to mess about, and when he produced the magic word *homoousios* ('of one substance', or 'one in Being') he found that most fell into line, even if only temporarily. He did probably underestimate the scale of the problem, and fairly quickly realised that keeping Arius in exile was not sustainable. But he could be ruthless when he wanted to be. A new book by Harold Drake presents Constantine as an enthusiast for religious toleration, and the bishops as the ruthless ones who took advantage of the new situation.[10] I suspect both sides were equally ready to get what they could out of it. But in any case 'ecumenical' in the fourth century did not mean quite what it does today. It meant simply 'worldwide', and this was the first council that deliberately set out to be universal. In that however it was more hopeful than successful. The emperor provided travel expenses and accommodation, but still most of the attendance was from the east, and it was the east where there were most who later came to be regarded as Arian. Soon quite a lot of mythology attached to the meaning of the Council of Nicaea: for instance the total number who attended is unclear, but later writers claimed that it was 318, the same as the number of servants of Abraham.

The main subject at issue was christology, and specifically the relation of the Son to the Father. This was not of course new. However the very emphatic and repetitive first section of our Creed reflects the degree of contemporary debate; it goes further and is more explicit than early christological statements, even if it is less convoluted than some other contemporary ones. It is easy for us to forget how much was still fluid in the early fourth century. Nowadays we look back on Nicaea from the vantage point of the year 2001 as the first of the ecumenical councils, and if we forget that our Creed originated then we have been reminded of it by the heading in the ASB. But what differentiated it most for contemporaries was probably the fact that it had been called by the emperor: nothing could be the same again after that.

Contrary to what is commonly said, Constantine did not make Christianity the 'official' religion of the Roman empire, but those bishops who were on the right side could now indeed (and this was a momentous change) expect advancement, position and even wealth. Even so, Constantine's exhortations did not stop people from trying to get round the agreed formula, and later imperial interventions were not all so effective or longlasting. His son Constans tried again in 343 at Serdica (Sofia), but the easterners went off in a huff because Athanasius had been invited.[11] In their absence the Council produced a statement which Kelly describes as 'extreme and highly provocative',[12] after which a letter had to be sent to the Pope reassuring him that the intention was not to overturn the Creed of Nicaea, only to explain it more fully. It would be tedious to go into all the swings of opinion during the 56 years that separate the Councils of Nicaea and Constantinople. Constantius II, who ruled until 361, tried as hard as his father to sort things out, but his sympathies were on the opposite side, and the long statement produced in his presence at Sirmium in 357 explicitly objected to the use of the term *homoousios*, supposedly because it was not scriptural. The real reason becomes clear however in what followed: 'No one is ignorant that it is Catholic doctrine that there are two Persons of the Father and the Son, and that the Father is greater and the Son subordinated to the Father.'[13] Bishop Hilary of Poitiers referred to this creed as 'the Blasphemy', and that name has stuck. But it can be paralleled by several other creeds of the period, all in competition with each other.

Interestingly enough, in the light of the recent discussion in Synod about the translation of '*ek*', there was no mention in the original Nicene Creed of the Holy Spirit in connection with the conception of Christ. The Holy Spirit comes in only briefly at the end, in the baptismal formula. But by 381 there has been a big change. Now the whole paragraph about the work of the Holy Spirit is added, as well as the very phrase 'from the Holy Spirit and the Virgin Mary' on which Synod spent so much time.[14] The new emphasis was perhaps again a response to a current issue, designed clearly to reject the views of the so-called 'Spirit-fighters' who denied that the Spirit partook of the divine nature and argued that he was a creature, but the formulation was by no means new. Its addition shows us very clearly just how much the Creed was stitched together from different sources. Together with the final paragraph this replaces the original anathemas at the end of the Nicene Creed. There were other changes too: 'before all ages' removed any suggestion that there was a time before Christ was 'begotten'; 'of whose kingdom there will be no end' implicitly rejects the theories of Marcellus and Apollinaris, and so on. In fact our Creed is not a straight enlargement of the original Nicene, but a more complicated variant and a kind of composite.

There is also a problem as to when and how our present Creed actually originated. By the time of the Council of Chalcedon in 451 it was held that this was the creed of the Council held in Constantinople in 381, and that is how it is usually regarded and often described. However, there are some difficult technical points which seem to make this unlikely.[15] But if it is not the creed authorised by the Council of 381, then we don't know how or when it did come into being, or why we only hear about it in 451, when it was quoted in the Acts of the Council of Chalcedon. It is possible, in fact, that it was used liturgically as a baptismal creed, and this seems to be the case after 451.[16] If so, then this is probably how it found its way for the first time into the eucharistic liturgy, a context and use quite different from the history of creeds so far. But this obscurity only goes to show again – despite all the creeds and arguments of the mid-fourth century – how incomplete our knowledge of the history of our Creed really is. And after Chalcedon we are pretty well in the dark again until the sixth-century references – again extremely few.

I confess to finding the reports of the Synod discussions about the translation of 'ek' quite intriguing, not least because this phrase is actually one of the additions to the Nicene original. In the Acts of Chalcedon and again in a decree of Justinian in 533, the phrase 'from the Holy Spirit and the Virgin Mary' is assumed to have been added with a purpose, and again a polemical one: to reject implicitly the teachings of Apollinaris who was regarded as denying the full humanity of Christ.[17] But this is another thing on which one can't be certain. The phrase was not new; for instance it seems to have been in the Roman creed, and 'from the Holy Spirit from the Virgin Mary' comes in the *Apostolic Traditions* of Hippolytus (third century).[18] But perhaps it is also relevant that in the late fourth century the details of the Virgin birth were being debated (for example by St Jerome and St Ambrose) in a degree of detail not contemplated even at the time of Nicaea. This happened not simply in the context of Christology but even more in the context of discussions of virginity and celibacy, and it makes good sense for these words to appear here. As several people pointed out in the Synod debate, 'from' is not so important as 'and', which recognises the two natures of Christ in the Incarnation. It was argued that without 'and' Mary's role appears purely passive, and (I quote) 'that this may demean the place of women in the economy of creation and of redemption'.[19] However what we must *not* do, as one letter-writer in the *Church Times* pointed out, is try to impose twenty-first century ideas on the fourth-century wording.[20] Against change, it was argued that Anglicans receive their doctrine through the liturgy, and that we received the Creed from the Prayer Book, not from the so-called 'original Greek'.[21] Still, addition or not, 'from' and 'and' are indeed better translations of the Greek text as presented at Chalcedon in 451, and anti-Apollinarian or no, they have found their way into the new texts.

In chronological terms, and in terms of the amount of evidence available, there seems to be a big gap in knowledge of our Creed between the Council of Chalcedon, with its endorsement of the 318 Fathers of Nicaea and the 150 Fathers of Constantinople, and the safe haven of universal acceptance into the Eucharist. A great flurry of information, in the 'age of synodal creeds', is followed by hardly anything. Perhaps it was used liturgically here and there, but that's as much as we can say. But it certainly did not win immediate acceptance. Chalcedon itself was rejected, and continued to be rejected, by large parts of the east, though again it took time before one could begin to speak of a 'Monophysite' church organisation. Our picture of the great

councils is very much based on the hindsight of later centuries – impressions at the time would have been very
different.

Slow and hesitant though the process was in practice,
for us the incorporation of our Creed into the eucharistic
liturgy seems like the end of the story. Yet we must not
imagine that discussion stopped. On the contrary, what
did happen after Chalcedon was that the agenda shifted.
Arianism was now in the past, though the term kept on
recurring as a term of abuse. Emperors after Chalcedon
were still desperate to unite east and west, but the issue
was now that of the divine nature – two natures, as agreed
at Chalcedon, or one, divine, nature, as large numbers
of eastern Christians passionately believed. They did not
succeed in solving the issue, and Justinian's great council
called to win over the east in 553 had the result of alienating
the Italian church. But a succession of Greek popes in the
seventh century meant that Rome and Constantinople were
still united. When the emperors of the mid-seventh century
tried to enforce another compromise, the doctrine of 'one
will' in Christ, the Roman church stood firm and supported
the orthodox Chalcedonian opposition (as a result Pope
Martin and Maximus Confessor were put on trial and went
to their deaths). Also in the seventh century, there was
much debate as to whether Christ really suffered – it being
argued that God cannot suffer; and this too was the subject
of conciliar debate. Even during the Iconoclastic period in
the eighth and ninth centuries, when it was imperial policy
to destroy images and attack their theological justification,
Rome was fully behind the iconophiles whose side eventually won the argument. Again the basis was christological
– could the divine nature be depicted? Was Christ in his
human form a creature? All these debates produced statements of faith, quite often known like our Creed as
'symbols', and usually attached to sets of anathemas
against those on the other side of the argument.

About our Creed's use in the eucharistic liturgy, we really
know very little. A sixth-century source tells us quite
laconically in separate passages that it was used by a
Monophysite patriarch of Antioch and a patriarch of
Constantinople of similar views. This seems rather sur-

prising, though he also indicates that at Constantinople anyway it was only used once a year.[22] Whatever the circumstances, the passionate public interest in these issues in Constantinople in the early sixth century made it controversial – it is a bit hard for us to imagine it, but this was a time when slogans about Christology were shouted in the streets. The Emperor Anastasius was thought to have Monophysite views and was shouted at in the streets and the Hippodrome, and under the orthodox Emperor Justinian the crowd shouted Monophysite slogans during the meetings he was holding to try to bring the parties together:[23] 'Augustus Justinian, may you be victorious; destroy, burn the document issued by the bishops of the Synod of Chalcedon.' We are not exactly in a safe haven as yet. There was also a question as to the Creed's position in the liturgy – after the offertory and before the Peace, or, as the emperor ordered in 568, before the Lord's Prayer. Uncertainty surrounds what actually happened. Even the decree of Justin II in 568 is only known from a western (Spanish) chronicler.[24] Nevertheless, the emperor's publicist incorporated the terminology of the Creed into the poem he wrote in Constantinople to celebrate Justin's accession, and the same emperor issued a decree about the faith in 572 as part of a crackdown against Monophysites in which he explicitly said that he was guided by the 'holy symbol', i.e. the Creed.[25] Admittedly there was no new 'official' Creed. But these were hotly debated issues, and I really would not like to assume that there was any uniformity of practice. And the argument seems to have focused on the status of councils rather than on Creeds as such: Creeds were, as it were, the outward sign of the status of the councils in question. Knowledge of history was also becoming polarised, and many apparently authoritative statements from this period about the previous history of orthodox doctrine turn out to be extremely one-sided. For example, in an edict issued shortly afterwards the councils to which Justin refers have been telescoped into only Nicaea, Constantinople and Ephesus, with no mention of Chalcedon (a deliberate omission for reasons of tact). As for the liturgy as it was celebrated on a regular basis, the truth is that we know next to nothing about what actually happened in the liturgy in churches outside Constantinople and Jerusalem, and not much in detail even there.

I think this puts a rather different complexion on what is usually said about the *filioque* – the Latin word in the phrase in our Creed about the procession of the Holy Spirit 'from the Father and the Son', which is not part of the Creed as it appears in the Acts of Chalcedon. Although it is known from the Visigothic (Spanish) Council of Toledo in 589, the phrase appeared in the west in a rather *ad hoc* manner, not as a unified action by Rome and the west to change or add to the Creed in its agreed form. It was not unnatural that it did appear in the west however, for the greatest influence on western, Latin theology was Augustine, and the *filioque* is Augustinian. But Augustine, of course, was a closed book to the Greek-speaking east. We hear about the *filioque* again in a Frankish context at the end of the eighth century, by when it had come to eastern attention through its importation into a Frankish monastery in Jerusalem and aroused predictable objections. Our Creed preserves the western, local, version, not the wording in the Acts of Chalcedon. If we are 'going back to the original Greek', is it not logical to omit it?

It is time to turn back to the Creed as it is said today. In the process of writing this paper I have come to realise very forcibly just how much our Creed really is a historical document. An important function of the liturgy is to preserve memory, the collective memory of the Church, and this applies in large measure to the Creed. The danger, though, is that most of us have forgotten what that memory really relates to. As a historian, I can't help regretting that, and as a person deeply interested in the history of Christianity I can't help regretting it either. But more important, perhaps, than memory, for many people anyway, is that the Creed is a badge of identity. It marks us off, and it stakes a claim, just as it did when it was first composed. For all its faults and curiosities, it is the outward symbol of unity, used by churches not unified in other respects. Like an *entr'acte*, it also marks a moment within the Eucharist when the liturgy moves on to the next stage. Like it or not, we seem to be stuck with it. To give it up would be unthinkable – but also dangerous. What would a 'modern'

Creed look like? And by what process would it be agreed? Imperfect though it certainly is if approached as a statement of contemporary faith, a twenty-first century 'symbol', the present Creed, very importantly for Anglicans, reminds us of our early tradition. It reminds us that we do make claim to apostolic tradition; that we are indeed, not just *a*, but *the* Church. It reminds us that the Church's past was also imperfect. Conveniently for us as Affirming Catholics, it reminds us that the tradition we lay claim to is a catholic tradition, even if that word is misunderstood in its context in the Creed by many of those who say it. But it also challenges us to ask what the liturgy is really about, and what we are doing when we recite these words.

Having written this paper and actually having thought about the Creed in a way in which I don't think I had ever done before, I have lost my embarrassment at saying it. Of course I am an academic, and so I am likely to feel better once I have done some research on a problem. But I do think a little knowledge helps. And I do passionately feel that people need some explanation.

I ask myself what kind of understanding of the Church is revealed by this reflection on the Creed's formation and reception. Certainly no rosy, idealistic image. Those councils, and the many synods that went with them, the lobbying, yes, the deliberate falsification, the seeking after influence and position – all this is just as dirty and just as coats-off as any modern political battle. The protagonists were no strangers to the importance of the media. Other factors entered into this too: the religious inclination and personal competence of individual emperors was enormously important, and so were some of the colourful characters who dominated these struggles. The Church was formed in struggle, whether that struggle was founded in persecution or in the effort to get agreement, and this should be helpful to us in our own struggles. We do not have to believe that the working of the Holy Spirit necessarily made everything clear and easy.

Once we realise that our Creed is an imperfect production, stitched together from disparate elements, I think it becomes a little easier to understand. The repetitive, insistent, christological parts speak of a defining moment in the history of the Church, and for all the hesitations that one might have about the alliance of church and state, they still speak of a powerful and in the long term a successful effort to produce something on which all could agree. The formulaic repetition of the sequence of the life, death and resurrection of Christ by the assembled congregation brings them into the community and reiterates its basis. The last two paragraphs in one sense speak of fourth-century concerns, but they do so by incorporating the threefold terminology that had been used from the New Testament onwards. Our Creed came together in particular circumstances in the fourth century, and only gradually gained the position it holds today as the central statement of faith. But it is made from elements and phraseology which go back recognisably to apostolic and sub-apostolic times. Seen in that light, and with some understanding of how it developed, the Creed can indeed stand as a personal statement of acceptance of the central truths of creation, incarnation and hope of resurrection. Like the simpler Apostles' Creed, it contains the basic threefold affirmations of Christian belief, in God the Father, God the Son and God the Holy Spirit, and above all, what Paul calls 'God's own proof of his love towards us', the saving action of God through the Lord Jesus Christ.[26]

I return to the opening words: 'I believe'. We no longer live in an age sensitive to nuances of doctrine, and when we try to grasp them we usually go astray. But what does a Christian have to believe, and what could the Early Church agree on? John's gospel puts it at its simplest: John was sent 'that all men might believe' (1:7); Jesus' disciples 'believed' in him after the miracle at Cana (2:11); many 'believed' when they saw him in Jerusalem (2:23); 'whoever believes in the Son of Man shall have eternal life' (3:15). 'Belief' is belief in Jesus as the Christ, in the words of Ephesians 'one Lord, one belief [one faith], one baptism' (4:5). Despite all its complications, this is also what our Creed is trying to tell us.

Notes

1 R. P. C. Hanson, 'The achievement of orthodoxy in the fourth century AD', in Rowan Williams, ed., *The Making of Orthodoxy. Essays in Honour of Henry Chadwick* (Oxford, 1989), pp. 142–56, at p. 154.
2 J. N. D. Kelly, *Early Christian Creeds*, 3rd ed. (London, 1972), ch. 2.
3 Kelly, ibid. pp. 79, 85.
4 Hanson, op. cit., p. 153.
5 Virginia Burrus, ' "In the theatre of this life": the performance of orthodoxy in late antiquity', in William E. Klingshirn and Mark Vessey, eds., *The Limits of Ancient Christianity. Essays on Late Antique Thought and Culture in Honor of R. A. Markus* (Ann Arbor, 1999), pp. 80–96.
6 Vincent of Lérins, *Commonitorium* 2.5 (CCSL, pp. 64, 149).
7 R. A. Markus, 'The problem of self-definition: from sect to church', in id., *From Augustine to Gregory the Great* (London, 1983), no. I, at 7.
8 Kelly, op. cit., p. 206.
9 *VC* III.21; J. Stevenson, *A New Eusebius*, rev. W. H. C. Frend (London, 1987), no. 293.
10 H. A. Drake, *Constantine and the Bishops. The Politics of Intolerance* (Baltimore, 1999).
11 Kelly, op. cit., pp. 274–5.
12 Ibid. p. 278.
13 J. Stevenson, *Creeds, Councils and Controversies. Documents Illustrative of the History of the Church*, AD 337–461 (London, 1972, corr. 1873), no. 23.
14 Ibid. no. 220 for the two versions; Kelly, op. cit., ch. 10.
15 Clearly summarised in S. G. Hall, *Doctrine and Practice in the Early Church* (London, 1991), pp. 167–71.
16 Kelly, op. cit., pp. 344–5.
17 Ibid. p. 334.
18 Ibid. pp. 114–5, cf. p. 146.
19 See *The Times*, 15 Feb. 2000.
20 Revd David Percy, *Church Times*, July 1999.
21 *Church Times*, 6 Aug. 1999.
22 Kelly, op. cit., p. 348.
23 *Chron. Pasch.*, p. 629.
24 Joh. Biclar., *PL* 72, 863.
25 Corippus, *In laudem Iustini*, IV.297 ff.; Evagr., *HE* V.4.
26 Rom. 5:8.

6 The Prayers of the People*

Jack Nicholls

One of the little games I play when visiting the parishes of the Diocese of Sheffield is to compare the length of time taken for the Sermon, the Prayers of the People and the notices. Not infrequently the notices win by a considerable margin, but often the Prayers of the People come a close second. We are treated to Cook's tour of the world's trouble spots sometimes with a not too objective political commentary and then to vast amounts of information about individuals and their troubles suggesting, as Robert Runcie used to say, that God has 'temporarily mislaid His omniscience'. This is doubly frustrating when the person leading the prayers does so in such a personal way that the implication is that public prayer is private prayer writ large. In other words, we are treated to the personal feelings and attitudes of the individual in such a way that very few, if any, of those present, save the speaker, can wholeheartedly say 'amen' to what is uttered!

However, in this chapter I will leave aside the practicalities and idiosyncrasies of intercession leading and concentrate on other aspects of our lives as people of prayer.

We come to God in prayer because of our need. 'Blessed are those who know their need of God' (Matt. 5:1). So Jesus begins the Beatitudes and so we begin our prayer, out of our need – *our* need. Listen to some words from Carl Jung:

> I admire you Christians, because when you see somebody hungry and thirsty you see Jesus. When you see somebody in prison or in hospital you see Jesus. When you see somebody

*© Jack Nicholls 2000

72

who is strange, a stranger or naked, you see Jesus. What I don't understand is that you don't see Jesus in your own brokenness. Why are the poor always outside of you? Can't you see they're inside of you; in your hunger and thirst? That you too are sick; that you too are imprisoned in your own fears or need for honour and power; that you too have strange things inside of you which you don't understand; that you too are naked?

Down the road from where I live in south west Sheffield is Phoenix House, a rehabilitation centre for those who suffer from drug addiction. When it first opened some years ago local residents objected and attempted to recruit the local vicar to their cause. This so infuriated him that he became the Chairman of the Houses Management Committee and eventually converted many of the local objectors into supporters. It was a remarkable piece of work. The philosophy of Phoenix House is framed in the entrance hall, it reads:

We are here because there is no refuge finally from ourselves. Until we confront ourselves in the eyes and hearts of others, we are running. Until we suffer them to know our secrets, we can know no safety from them. Afraid to know ourselves we can know no others. Where else but in our common ground can we find such a mirror. Here at last we can appear clearly to ourselves: not as the giant of our dreams, nor the dwarf of our fears, but as people; part of the whole with a share in its purpose. Here together we can take root and grow, not alone as in death but alive in ourselves and in others.

This should be a true description of every Christian community, but is it true of the one to which you belong?

Our need and our belonging are what we bring to God in the prayers of the people and because we are part of the whole we cannot but bring along the whole; the whole of life; the whole of the world; the whole of ourselves. A priest I know has just lost his marriage and his priesthood because he insisted on living in three worlds (at least); his priestly ministry was one; his wife and children another; and a hidden private third life. He compartmentalised his life and he fell, as Jesus said he would: 'A house divided against itself cannot stand', 'He (she) who has ears to hear, let him hear.' I was fortunate in knowing Mother Mary Clare of the Sisters of the Love of God, over a long number of years. I once took to her a particular dilemma. I was always forgetting to pray for people who asked for my prayers. 'Father will you pray for my mother, she is very ill.' 'Of course I will', I would reply as I said good morning to the queue leaving church on Sunday and then I would forget. Two weeks later, 'Thank you Father, thank you. Mother is much better and I am sure that your prayers made all the difference.' I never had the courage to confess, 'Well as a matter of fact I didn't pray for her, I forgot.' I just received the thanks and felt rather guilty. Mother Mary Clare laughed as only she could, 'Silly boy, when you go before God in prayer you cannot leave anything behind. You carry in your heart every person, every incident, every thought, every feeling you have ever had and as you lay yourself before God so you bring all the mess as well.' 'My prayer' she said 'is really one sentence. Here I am, what a mess.' So it is that we 'gather up the fragments that nothing be lost' when we bring ourselves before God in prayer.

Mother Mary Clare taught me many things, but chief of them was about the place of prayer. The foot of the cross is the place of prayer, the place where the love of God and the agony of the world meet. Here we stay with the world on our heart; here God receives our offering; here we are incorporated into the transforming and transfiguring body of Christ at the altar of the cross.

Being part of the prayer of the people is greatly demanding. To be who we are together at the foot of the cross with the whole world on our hearts is costly indeed, but how else can we share in and fulfil our vocation to be the Body of Christ? What greater mission is there in which to participate?

I was, for a number of years, the Warden of the Community of St Mary the Virgin, Wantage. Towards the end of my period of office on one of my regular overnight visits, I had begun to think about my final sermon to the Community. I was stuck and went to bed that evening with some uplifting volume to put me to sleep. Within minutes God spoke in his rather unusual and eccentric way. The bed collapsed from beneath me. It was late; the Great

Silence had begun and there was I on a broken bed. I am not noted for my do-it-yourself expertise, but I could not stay at that particular angle for the rest of the night. So I went to the library and collected a pile of large books with which to prop up the bed. I chose almost exactly the right number of books, propped up the base and returned to bed with just one volume over. It was a dusty old book of Russian icons. I flicked through the pages and my eyes fell on one particular icon. The book told me that this was a *Deesis* and fortunately went on to describe just what a *Deesis* is: an icon of Our Lord sitting in judgement. On his left is St John the Baptist, on his right Our Lady. Being Russian, Our Lady is not the young, pure virgin dressed in blue as are most western portrayals of her, but instead is a middle-aged peasant woman in warm russet-red. She looks tough as old boots and quite determined about something. I discovered that one of her titles, particularly associated with a *Deesis* in Russian, is Mary, Mother of the Damned. She, the tough peasant mother, and John the Baptist, looking his most unattractive and aesthetic, are there pleading before Christ for the damned and if you will forgive the expression, they will damned well not move until they get their way. That is intercession; that is, in the best sense, compassion; that is the prayer of the people; that is our longing, our thirst.

'Leaving heaven for the love of others is the acid test of spirituality', as Rowan Williams says in his biography of Teresa of Avila. But if our longing is the redemption, transformation, transfiguration of the world, it is only that because of his longing for us. 'I thirst' said Jesus on the cross. The Hound of Heaven will not give up the chase and there is no escape. We long to share in his divinity, but will we allow him to find us and to catch us, to serve us and to love us into life – every part of us. Or do we cling on to part of our lives and foolishly try to refuse to take them with us into prayer and be transformed and transfigured by him in whose presence we pray. Some words from the Ascent of Mount Carmel come to mind:

> For it comes to the same thing whether a bird be held by a slender cord or by a stout one; since, even if it be slender, the

bird will be as well held as though it were stout, for so long as it breaks it not and flies not away. It is true that the slender one is easier to break; still, easy though it be, the bird will not fly away if it be not broken. And thus the soul that has attachment to anything, however much virtue it possesses, will not attain to the liberty of Divine union.

I don't know about you but it is heavy chains not slender threads which bind me. I know that I have a long way to go, but there is a sense in which this matters less than the fundamental fact of knowing my need of God and my fellowship in the Body of Christ with you – in other words, to be longing and to belong. This is what we take with us when we come before God with the people on our hearts in the prayers of the people.

Accompanying people to the foot of the cross, the place of intercession, was illustrated to me in my recent visit to Mount Athos. I stayed for two nights at the Monastery of Iveron where I was told that, as a non-Orthodox guest, I would not be permitted to enter the main body of the church during the Liturgy. I sat myself, therefore, in the middle of the night in the outermost cloister, feeling not a little disgruntled at being excluded – after all, I am a bishop of the Church of England! As I sat there I began, however, to change my mind as I realised how far I am from the heart of God. It seemed somehow right for me to be on the outside. I had been sitting with my thoughts for only a very few minutes when I was approached by one of the monks who beckoned me to move further in and sat me on a seat with a better view of the door into the main church. Scarcely had I settled there, when along came another monk and moved me yet further in. Finally, one of the older members of the Community came up to me and took me to the very door itself, where he sat me on a seat from which I could participate as fully as any outsider could in the Liturgy of the day. He then sat down beside me, in a seat with a worse view than I and remained there throughout the night. He would not go in because I could not go in. To stay and pray with the outsider who cannot enter is part of the cost of intercession.

Two days later, this time at the Monastery of St Panteleimon – the only Russian monastery on Mount Athos – I found myself similarly seated next to a poorly-looking Greek peasant. None of us looks our best at 2.30 am, but this man looked particularly ill. I had discovered earlier in the day that he was about to enter hospital for major heart surgery and he was clearly apprehensive at the prospect. After almost four hours, we came to the climax of the Liturgy, the Eucharistic Prayer, and as the prayer began a large bear-like Russian monk appeared from the gloom wearing, I have to say, what I can only describe as the dirtiest habit I have every seen. He spoke no Greek, the Greek spoke no Russian, but the monk took him under his arm and slowly walked him to the front of the church before the iconostasis. There they both knelt, the Russian with his arm around the Greek, until after Communion. The peasant was then returned to his seat next to me and he appeared as though he had just been to heaven. I believe he had been accompanied to the foot of the Cross where pain and love meet to be with the Christ whose death is proclaimed at each and every Eucharist.

Intercession is a costly calling and those of us who have the privilege of being called to lives of intercession, need to be aware of that cost.

Mount Athos is blessed with many beautiful icons and at the Monastery of Iveron an icon restorer has been employed to great effect. The guest master explained to me that although an icon is a window into heaven, very often the window has become overlaid by centuries of candle grease, dirt and by faded varnish or by the offerings of the faithful which take the form of silver plates which, nailed to the surface of the icon, obscure the original portrayal. Sometimes only the face of our Lord or one of his saints remains and even this is too faded to recognise. The skilled icon restorer removes the plates without destroying the icon and cleans the varnish, the dirt and the grease of centuries of religion to reveal the pristine window into God. The guest master simply said, 'We all need an icon restorer.' How right he was and if we are to be faithful to our calling to accompany others to the foot of the cross, we need to be constantly aware of our own need.

Maybe the most famous icon in the western world is

Rublev's *Hospitality of Abraham*, that remarkable depiction of the Trinity. You will recall that the three angels sit round three sides of the table inviting the observer to participate in the life of God, to be a guest at the table of the Kingdom. There in the centre of the table is a chalice and orthodox iconographers often portray the chalice as the cross. In fact, often a cross is to be seen within the chalice. We are called to participate in the life of the Cross; we are called to receive the chalice which Jesus received.

Icons of the Passion[1] is a remarkable little book based on a series of woodcarvings. It is similar but not quite the same as the Stations of the Cross. Each woodcarving is accompanied by a meditation by Bill Vanstone, who died in 1999. The book has just been reissued as a memorial to Bill. The first carving depicts Jesus in Gethsemane. His hands are lifted well above his head and he is in the act of receiving a chalice. The words are as follows:

> All lovers comes at last to Gethsemane, and wait there for the outcome of their loving. Loving itself is a beginning, an invitation, an offering: for the receiving which it invites but does not compel love can only wait, and to wait no longer is to cease to love.
>
> For the receiving or the rejection, the understanding or the misunderstanding, the loving or the grudging response, love must wait: and the intensity of the waiting is the measure of the loving. As He waits who is the all-loving, the sweat falls like drops of blood; and His hands tremble as they reach up to take and receive the cup of the world's response.
>
> What is in the cup cannot be seen. But because he does not cease to love, he will wait for whatever comes. His hands will always be upraised to receive and take to himself whatever is mixed in the cup which contains the world's response.

Maybe the next time the minister says 'Let us pray' our 'Yes' should be whispered.

Notes

1 W. H. Vanstone, *Icons of the Passion*, 2nd ed., (London: Darton, Longman and Todd, 2000).

7 The Great Thanksgiving Prayer*

Frances Young

I want to offer this as a tribute to Gordon Wakefield who died on 11 September 2000. Some of you at any rate know about the significance of Gordon. He was, like me, a Methodist minister, and a very significant ecumenist. He was the first and only Methodist Principal of the ecumenical, theological training college in Birmingham, Queens. His most well known publication is *The Dictionary of Spirituality*, which he edited and which was published by SCM. Most significantly, he was a great liturgist of enormous influence in the Joint Liturgical Group, which produced the lectionaries which we commonly follow.

1. The Recovery of the Great Prayer of Thanksgiving – the Liturgical Movement

I am not a liturgist, but as a Methodist I grew up with a communion liturgy based on the *Book of Common Prayer*, and found myself overtaken by a new approach with the publication of the *Methodist Service Book* in the 1970s. My experience must parallel that of many of you as you have experienced the various experimental rites being incorporated into the *Alternative Service Book* of 1980. All of this was part of the so-called 'Liturgical Movement', a significant feature of which was the recovery of the *anaphora* from the liturgical texts of the Early Church, and the way that that influenced the development of a Great Thanksgiving

*© Frances Young 2000

Prayer in these newer liturgies. This is where I propose to begin.

The recovery of the Great Thanksgiving Prayer in western liturgies is one of the significant things of our time. The interesting question, however, is: was this recovery merely a kind of primitivism? After all, at the time the historico–critical thrust of scholarship was dominant. It is rather curious, then, that such an apparently Protestant return to origins accompanied the modernising of our language, the release from the King James version of the Bible, and so on. Furthermore, the liturgical movement was generated largely, I guess, among Catholics, which makes it even odder if it was simply a matter of a sort of primitivism. You will be aware of the considerable freedom which has been shown in the variety of texts composed for the Great Thanksgiving Prayer which are offered as options in the new *Methodist Service Book* and in the provisions of *Common Worship*. This suggests that we are not actually seeing a mere copying of the past, and yet the influence of scholarship in the development is very clear.

There are a few general points to be drawn from this. The first is that I think it is important we recognise how often a renaissance is linked with a return to sources, with a rediscovery of the past, seen in a new way. The second point is that the 'Liturgical Movement' was ecumenical, and it captured a catholicity with respect to eucharistic worship which is quite remarkable. Across the denominations, there are many variations of an increasingly similar basic pattern, and various elements that make up the great prayer. In 1991 I had the privilege (although before I went I was not sure it was going to be that) of going with the 'Faith and Light' movement on a pilgrimage to Lourdes. I was the preacher at an Anglican Eucharist at the upper Basilica at the Shrine, and then went to a celebration of the Roman Catholic Eucharist for English-speaking pilgrims: the services were virtually identical. The third point I would like to draw out is that this recovery has allowed the sacramental theology of eastern Christendom to dissolve some of the Reformation and post-Reformation hangups of the west. It is an interesting question why the West Syrian liturgy was so influential in the recovery of the

Great Thanksgiving Prayer, but at any rate it meant that a certain commonality with the Orthodox, who use the liturgies of St Chrysostom and St Basil, has become part of our worship.

Reference to the importance of return to sources brings to mind my membership of a small group of Methodists and Orthodox who have now met a couple of times in conference with the specific task of discovering our common spirituality on the basis of our sources. John Wesley's debt to the Fathers was considerably greater than might appear at first sight. At the last conference, in July 2000, a paper was given by an American Methodist scholar on the recovery of the Great Thanksgiving Prayer. There are one or two insights I drew from it which I would like to share. Of course, one of the things about the recovery of the Great Thanksgiving Prayer is that we have got an *epiclesis* back, a point which I shall return to later. Grant White writes in his opening paragraph:

> One day, after I had lectured on the *epiclesis* in Orthodox *anaphoras* and revised western Christian eucharistic prayers, one of my students (in his mid-20s) came up to me and said enthusiastically, 'Grant, the *epiclesis* rocks!'

I would also like to use his definition of the Great Prayer of Thanksgiving from the opening of his paper:

> It is the great prayer of thanksgiving in the liturgy of the Eucharist, in which, over bread and wine, the Christian assembly thanks God for creation and redemption, makes memorial of the saving work of God in Christ, and asks God to fulfil God's purposes for the cosmos through the action of the Holy Spirit.

Many have found the recovery of the Great Thanksgiving Prayer a significant enriching of their eucharistic experience, and it places us within a global, ecumenical community.

2. The Ancient Context and its Significance – Prayer, Thanksgiving, Sacrifice

If it is recovery which we are talking about, then maybe we would benefit from looking at the ancient context, and

81

the significance of prayer and thanksgiving and sacrifice in the world from which this tradition came. Christian worship did not emerge in a vacuum, but in a specific cultural context. The earliest Christians asserted that in the Eucharist they were offering bloodless sacrifice, and they contrasted this with the sacrifices of the religions of the world in which they lived. This was a world where religion, prayer and the offering of material gifts to the gods were inseparable. Let me quote myself as a way of sketching this for you:

Because they did not sacrifice to domestic, civic, or imperial gods and goddesses, Christians were dubbed atheists, like Epicurian philosophers. It was normal then for prayers to be accompanied by gifts. Clearly, people felt themselves to be part of a society which included supernatural beings who had an effect on their lives. And just as social transactions in most cultures are oiled by gifts, so commerce with these unseen powers had to be conducted in the same way. Thus, there are countless examples of a city or an individual in distress vowing to make rich offerings to some God if that divine person would render assistance immediately. It is not surprising that some scholars of previous generations spoke of such prayer as a *negotium* or business transaction. But this hardly does justice to the wide range of motivations that can be discerned. If you want to celebrate something you throw a party with lots of eats and drinks. If you want to express gratitude you give a box of chocolates, and gifts and greeting cards are associated with birthdays and retirements, in other words with honouring people. When many years ago my youngster broke our neighbour's window, reconciliation took the form of a visit, an apology and not merely restitution in repairing the window, but a bunch of flowers and a box of chocolates. It is such analogies which help us to appreciate the highly concrete expressions of prayer which sacrifice constituted.

In other words, many prayers may have been requests accompanied by the equivalent of bribery and corruption, but that kind of behaviour does not exhaust the notion of prayer. Thanksgiving, veneration, repentance, celebration, being in a relationship, or restoring relationships, dealing with guilt, impurity or alienation, getting rid of hostile or evil influences, buying off divine anger, or enjoying peace, love, joy and hope all of these things were involved in religious rites which expressed prayer to gods or demons.[1]

What I have described is very transactional in nature; but then we have to remember that in that society there was a kind of mutual obligation in structures of patronage, so that thanksgiving was a proper response to gift or support. It is very interesting to note that there was a convention of offering thanks to the gods at the opening of the letter, and if you look at Paul's letters you'll find that he does that too as part of a social convention. In the context of Christianity, we have to add in the background in the biblical covenant and note the importance of thanksgiving in epistles and prayer texts, such as the psalms.

I have beside me a book called *Prayer from Alexander to Constantine: A Critical Anthology*.[2] It includes Jewish examples from much material from the period, including the apocryphal texts, inter-testamental literature, the Dead Sea Scrolls, Philo, Josephus and the works of the Rabbis. Apart from the expected petitions and blessings, thanksgiving and recollection of acts of grace or salvation provide the dominant motif. Honouring God's name, praise and so on is closely related to the expression of gratitude. Let me share just one example (p. 104):

> Gladly have we received and stored up the gifts of nature. Yet we do not ever ascribe our keeping to any corruptible cause, but to God, the Creator and Father and Saviour of both the world and the things in the world, whose prerogative it is to nourish and carefully protect both through these and without these. Look at how he continually nourished our ancestors in their countless thousands as they traversed the trackless and totally barren desert for the life of a generation – forty years, as if they were in a most fertile and productive land. He cut open brand new springs for a generous supply of drinking water. He rained nourishment from Heaven.

The prayer concludes: 'They would care little for the supplies and marvel at and worship the Supplier, honouring him with appropriate hymns and benedictions.'

The memorial and the thanksgiving are closely connected in that Jewish example. In Greek and Roman texts we find

83

that invocations, petitions and hymns dominate, but thanks
for deliverance is also found in these texts. I quote from
one example, a Hermetic prayer of thanksgiving from the
corpus of material associated with the worship of Hermes
(p. 203):

> We give You thanks! Every soul and heart is stretched out to
> You, O name which cannot be troubled, honoured by the name
> 'God' and praised by the name 'Father' . . . The thanksgiving of
> the one who reaches to You is one thing: that we know You. We
> have known You.
>
>   O life of life, we have known You. O womb of every sowing,
> we have known You . . .

and so it continues. And so they are continually remembering this one they have known and they have one wish:
to be preserved in this knowledge. But fundamentally the
text is one of thanksgiving for the revelation which has
come.

The most pertinent early Christian text is the *Didache* (p.
263). This text refers to the Eucharist, telling how regarding
the cup 'we thank you, our Father for the holy vine', then
over the broken bread, 'we thank you, our Father, for life
and knowledge . . .' And then

> . . . after the meal this is how you are to give thanks: 'We thank
> you, Holy Father, for your holy name which you caused to dwell
> in our hearts, for knowledge, faith and immortality which you
> have made known to us through Jesus your servant. To you be
> glory forever. You, Master Almighty, have created all things for
> the sake of your name. Food and drink you have given to human
> beings for their refreshment, that they may give thanks to you.
> But us you have graced with spiritual food and drink, and
> eternal life, through your servant.'

So we find prayer in the ancient world accompanying a
thank offering, and I think it is very important that one of
the earliest Christian theologians, Irenaeus, spoke of the
Eucharist as a thank offering for the first fruits of the whole
of creation. In the work of Hippolytus we find the early
Christians making offerings, including gifts in kind, the
first fruits of everything being offered, doubtless because
Christians were located in this culture of giving thanks for

everything and accompanying it with gifts. There is this sense of obligation to God, of not taking anything for granted.

3. A Journey Through the Prayer

Having looked at that background from which emerges the Great Thanksgiving Prayer, let us take a journey through the form of the prayer itself. It is not verbally fixed, and yet it has a shape, a series of elements which vary in order, but which predominate, nevertheless.

The first element is, of course, the opening call, to lift up our hearts, the obligation to offer thanksgiving. I contrast this with the lack of gratitude and appreciation in modern life. The focus is all on our rights and our claims, on choice and freedom. We breathe in the constant atmosphere of complaint and objection to the conditions of life: 'It really shouldn't be allowed to happen that we suffer and are prone to accident, should it?' Thanksgiving is not natural for us in our culture. We need to foster it by putting our minds into contexts where thanksgiving is given priority, in exactly the way in which we do when we try to teach our children to say 'thank you' – encouraging the formation of habits which could potentially become more than habitual. Just a week or two ago, I heard someone speaking who had come to this country round about the time of the Second World War. He said that he did not know very much English when he arrived. The one phrase he knew was 'thank you very much'. So he went around saying thank you very much to everybody. After a bit somebody took him aside and said, 'you know you only say thank you very much when it's something really significant that has happened. You don't always need to say it.' So the next time somebody did something he said, 'Thank you, but not very much.'

It seems to me that in the Great Thanksgiving Prayer we are asserting a fundamental spiritual stance, a response to life, the universe and everything which is sheer gratitude and wonder. This stance is potentially immensely liberating. I shall never forget the moment when I discovered that I wanted to give thanks for my son Arthur, who was born with the most profound disabilities. It is immensely liberating to give thanks. So it is right to give him thanks and praise. Indeed it is our duty and our joy at all times and in all places. The basic response of thanksgiving is something that spills over into the whole of life. True, we do not always feel like that, but the Eucharist keeps us in remembrance that it is not about feelings: it is about a whole perspective on reality which requires this response, because we are creatures who owe everything to our Creator, and we are making a thank offering. Let me remind you, too, that this making of a thank offering is one way in which the Eucharist is a sacrifice, the sacrifice of the best we have and the best we can be.

At the heart, it is the first fruits of the creation according to Irenaeus, a key reference point for the new eucharistic services but a radical departure from the *Book of Common Prayer*. The Eucharist, as centred in the Great Thanksgiving Prayer, is not just about atonement or spiritual feeding, or Real Presence. It is about the whole overarching narrative which gives us a sense of our place in things, beginning with creation. There are two comments I would like to make about this. The first is to underline the sacramental nature of the whole of creation, as Irenaeus stressed in his association of the Eucharist with the first fruits. Anything and everything may mediate God to us. The Eucharist takes the ordinary things of life and enables their transfiguration so that they resonate with the divine. Many years ago, my younger brother, who died at the age of 16, but already felt a call to ministry, commented that Methodists should celebrate the Eucharist with a cup of tea and a bun, because it is fundamentally taking the ordinary things of life and transfiguring them; and Methodists, as you probably know, enjoy cups of tea and buns.

My second comment is on being a creature. The trouble is that we have overreached our creaturely status. As a race, humankind suffers from hybris, from that pride and challenge to the gods which is at the very heart of much Greek tragedy. If we look at the biblical narratives, Adam is the classic example, but I also think of Cain and Abel, of the Tower of Babel, and many other pointers to this same truth that Greek tragedy explored. I have been working on

Cyril of Alexandria recently. I think it is clear that he has a very particular way of reading the Bible which sees the narratives as one exemplar after another of both individual and corporate failure, of falling short, of disobedience, of this kind of self-aggrandisement which is somehow at the root of human life, this seeking to be equal with God, to climb the heavens. This Fall is followed by restoration through the grace of God.

It seems to me that one difficulty for us in our cultural context is the resistance to this analysis of the human condition. We are surrounded by an optimistic belief that we only have to find the right formula and anything can be put right. Even death can be cheated. Certainly, we could end poverty and war if we only went about it the right way. The huge success of scientific medicine, the fact that we live twice as long as we used to live on average, and that our life conditions have been hugely transformed have encouraged this belief that we can create Utopia. Perhaps the twentieth century challenged many aspects of nineteenth century optimism, and by the end of it socialism failed and the Soviet bloc imploded; but we should remember that that was a huge experiment in establishing Utopia. This utopian quest is sometimes mirrored in our Christian rhetoric about the kingdom of God. Find the right formula and we put the whole world to rights – a view analagous to the view which we see expressed in the popular press that somehow we could bring death to an end tomorrow if we only had the right medicine.

On all kinds of grounds, the biblical story of the Fall has ceased to ring true. People think that it is inconsistent with evolution, that it has been overtaken by psychology and genetics, and that, in particular, it does enormous damage to people because it creates guilt complexes. Nonetheless, if we look around realistically at the world we live in, does it not in fact ring true? *Corruptio optimi pessima*, the worst thing is the corruption of the best things. And there is a sense in which our wisdom, our knowledge is so easily corrupted. Science, one of the wonders of the human endeavour, produces the atom bomb. And who knows what genetic modification will bring.

One of the fascinating things which I have been pursuing

lately is the imagery used to depict wisdom in the Bible. Do you realise that the snake, the serpent is a symbol of wisdom? In that light let's reconsider the story in the Book of Numbers about the Israelites suffering from snakebite: are they not bitten by an attack of worldly wisdom? How much better it would have been to go back to the fleshpots of Egypt! And wasn't it just common sense, the better part of worldly wisdom was to go back to Egypt, even if it did mean going back to slavery, when here they were in the desert, dying of hunger and thirst? The antidote to that is the bronze serpent, the divine wisdom which John's gospel sees as incarnate in Jesus. People get life by looking up at the antidote to the snakebites of worldly wisdom. There was an occasion when I was cycling in France and came across a very tumble-down church. In one of the transepts, or side-chapels, which was not actually open to the sky and sprouting vegetation, there was a marvellous, very modern crucifix which was made of two bits of wood, one dark, one light, stuck together. On the Cross hung an extremely curvaceous, coil-like figure of Christ. I suddenly realised I was looking at the serpent Christ, the bronze serpent raised up in the desert, and if you look at it, you will find the antidote.

The whole story of creation, fall and redemption is set out in the Great Thanksgiving Prayer. This is the shaping, the sense-making narrative, which gives us the content of our thanksgiving and makes sense of our lives. The thanksgiving is not merely sentimental or superficial. This prayer just does not allow that. It is a full-frontal facing up to the awful realities of sin, death and the judgement of God. Without a sense of gone-wrongness, of being part of corporate and individual failure, that deep sense of thanksgiving for redemption is not possible. It requires a depth of humility which I suspect a lot of our do-gooding, activist fellow Christians lack. It requires a perspective on oneself and humanity, which is not a wallowing in guilt. Guilt is essentially self-centred and so what is properly being drawn out of us is a profound receptivity, a recognition that we are not self-sufficient; but that we are all needy, and that we kneel alongside many others who are needy in their turn.

88

In this vein, I have been much struck by the symbolism of Mary as the type of the Church. Mary, in her humility and receptivity, enabled the birth of Christ into the world. And what does the Magnificat mean? It means that the humble are lifted up. It is characteristic of the rich and the powerful to be in control, and the temptation of the do-gooder is to be in control. That is not the way of the Magnificat. The Magnificat requires humility and waiting upon God. This waiting leads to worship. So we come to the Sanctus. Of course this is evidence that at the heart of Christian worship is the notion that somehow the worship of heaven is mirrored on earth. It comes from Isaiah 6 and the Book of Revelation, and it points to the Communion of Saints, nay more to the whole creation, angelic and earthly. We are taken up into something which is beyond ourselves. This is not about me, it's not about my church, my fellowship. It is about the whole of God's creation in eternity, and it potentially blows apart all exclusive claims. I often think about the hubris of those who think they have got God in their pockets – the sort who believe that if they pray there will be a free parking space somewhere in town. If we really believe in God, who is the God of the whole universe, then that blows all that sort of thing apart. What is more, it blows apart any exclusive feelings we may have about non-believers, Jews, Muslims, people of other faiths. Dare we deny that they belong to the whole of God's creation? It is God's business, not ours, how others will find their *eschaton*, singing in the choir, or playing in the orchestra of praise and thanksgiving. And does it not perhaps make us wonder about that difficult doctrine of providence? At the very least is that not saying something about learning to live as if this is all God's gracious gift? In the Benedictus we turn to welcoming one who comes in the name of the Lord. The worship which mirrors the worship of Heaven is only possible because of the descent, because of the emptying, the *kenosis*, the accommodating to our level of the transcendent God. This is a perennial theme of many of the Early Church Fathers. It is almost as though Cyril of Alexandria is talking about the *kenosis* as a kind of mirroring of our Fall so that we might rise and be redeemed.

Now it is the turn of the institution narrative, the memorial of Christ's Passion, the *anamnesis*. This narrative is telling us where we have come from, who we are and where we are going to. We are reminded of our history; and it strikes me how important it is that we repeatedly rehearse this in order to claim our identity, to understand it, to articulate it and appropriate it. It is here, of course, that we come to other notions of sacrifice affecting the reality of what we are doing: the covenant sacrifice. The covenant between God and his people is renewed and completed in the new covenant in Christ. This covenant is sealed in the atoning sacrifice of Christ offered for the sins of the whole world. It seems to me absolutely vital that we forget any theories which advance the case for a sacrifice which is replayed. As John Chrysostom said, 'There is only one sacrifice, the sacrifice of Christ.' It is not so much replayed as *realised* in us and for us in a multiplicity of Eucharists. The cross and the resurrection are at the heart of a kind of typology which reverses the Fall with the redemption.

The rite moves on to the offering of ourselves, offered as a living sacrifice. Yes, we offer the elements as the first fruits of creation; but alongside them we offer ourselves. We offer spiritual sacrifices, and we seek sanctification of these offerings. In this representation of what Christ has done we are brought to a conviction of the heart which enables that miracle of sanctification often to happen. As the hymn puts it,

> Love so amazing, so divine,
> Demands my soul, my life, my all.

Any consideration of our sanctification leads us to consider the importance of the *epiclesis*. This portion of the thanksgiving is placed at different points in the many versions of the Great Thanksgiving Prayer. Sometimes, the invocation concentrates upon the work of the Holy Spirit in bringing about the sanctification of the Body of Christ in the sense of the community rather than the Body of Christ in the sense of the elements. Ideally, the invocation combines the two. What I consider to be perhaps the most important thing about the *epiclesis*, however, is that it places the Trinity at the very heart of the dynamic of this ritual remembering which makes real for us what Christ has done. Through the sanctifying of the offering the sanctification of the participants can take place: we are equipped and nourished for life by this spiritual feeding. In this dynamic of love we are joining in a communion sacrifice in a double sense. Many sacrifices in the ancient world were great parties in which the god was invited to come and celebrate with all the people who were there, and they had a great feast, and the only time they ever ate meat was when they sacrificed. So it was a communion sacrifice in the presence of God, but also a communion in the sense of spiritual feeding, and that inevitably brings us on to the question of the transformation of the elements.

4. Some Thoughts on Real Presence and the Body of Christ

In the light of this survey of the prayer, let us go on to think about Real Presence and the Body of Christ. The debate focused by the Reformation was very much a dispute about the elements and their transformation: whether or not the elements became the Body and Blood of Christ in any substantive rather than merely spiritual sense. Alongside this there has been a lasting debate about the community as a whole, the Body of Christ in the world. The work of modern ecumenists like Gordon Wakefield has highlighted for the whole Church the true authority of the *laos*, the People of God made in Baptism and formed by the Eucharist. This redressing of the balance away from sacerdotalism raises the question of whether the priest represents Christ in a unique and mediating way, and if so in what sense? I did some work at one point on the whole notion of priesthood in typology, and the claim in some catholic traditions that a woman could not be a priest because a woman could not represent Christ. I think that it is very important to underline here that we are not talking about a Passion play, any more than we are talking about a repeat of Christ's sacrifice. We are all called to be types of Christ. In the ancient Church, martyrs, women and men were types of Christ. And there is a very real sense in which the priest is simply a representative person of the whole community being the Body of Christ. The Real Presence is where two or three are gathered together, where the *anamnesis* makes real and effective what Christ did once for all on the cross.

The classic debates about the Eucharist reduce the significance of symbolism and literalise a particular outmoded scientific theory, posited by Aristotle and recapitulated from the Middle Ages. These debates reduce the dynamic of the ritual. The dynamic of the ritual depends upon the sacralising of particular things in a communal rite. I think Mary Douglas in her book *Purity and Danger* put her finger on the really important thing. Using the form of a parable, she makes the point that in sacrifice what people did was take all the taboo and terrible things of life and put them in a ritual context so that they were sacralised. Her parable was that of the gardener pulling up all the weeds in the garden, cleansing the garden of all these horrible things which were not part of the beauty of it. He put all the nasty weeds on the compost heap so that as they composted they were able to give new life, dug back into the garden. The sacrificial rituals she saw as being a way, somehow, of facing up to those awful things, and somehow turning them into something that is life-giving and holy. Now, no priest can do this on his or her own with some kind of magic. You need the whole people of God celebrating the Eucharist. Being a Methodist, I have to quote Charles Wesley:

> Who thy mysterious supper share,
>   here at thy table fed,
> Many and yet but one we are,
>   One undivided bread.
> One, with the living bread divine,
>   Which now by faith we eat,
> Our hearts and minds and spirits join,
>   And all in Jesus meet.
> His presence makes the feast;
>   And now our spirits feel
> The glory not to be expressed,
>   The joy unspeakable.

I remember during my training for ordination, going to an inner-city church for Easter. For the first time I was involved in being the pastor, and in helping with the Easter Communion. The inner-city church somehow exploded all the barriers in human society. It was multi-racial; it had people with all kinds of different ways of being Christian. There were young and old; working men and some more educated people; people from different classes and backgrounds. I can still remember the moment of going around for the first time, putting the bread in the hands of people, who held them out. I noticed how all their hands were so different. It was there that I almost joined in that vision of Isaiah, and saw the Lord high and lifted up in the midst of his temple. As the Body of Christ we are, in some mysterious way, a bit like the central nervous system. Christ is the head, and through our intercession and our being in the world, we transmit the messages to the head. We are the Body of Christ and intercession is incorporated into the Great Prayer.

Conclusion

So in the Eucharist, ordinary things are transfigured, and the overarching, or credal, narrative is realised in our worship. We proclaim what is most true in and about all creation and we cannot be unchanged by what is proclaimed. Grant White in his paper on the 'Recovery of the Great Thanksgiving Prayer in the Wesleyan Tradition'[3] referred to a small, United Methodist congregation in South Bend, Indiana, which began to celebrate the Eucharist as its main service every Sunday in the 1970s. He goes on:

> Shortly after beginning the weekly Eucharist, the congregation (which exists in an economically impoverished neighborhood), came to the conclusion that they could not share the feast of the Lord's body and blood every week while neglecting the hunger of the people around them in the neighborhood. And so began a meal prepared by the congregation members, served every Sunday immediately after the liturgy. Intended as another occasion of *koinonia* (in this instance between the congregation members and the members of the neighborhood), it flowed

93

directly from the experience and practise of the eucharistic *koinonia*. The congregation rightly saw the one as following from the other, as do their other ministries in and beyond the neighborhood.

John Wesley spoke of the Eucharist as a converting ordinance. Whether that means that we should have open communion, as Methodists have generally interpreted it, is controversial. Wesley was definitely right in the sense that it is a change of heart, a *metanoia*, which is at the heart of what happens in the Eucharist. Humility and gratitude lie at the heart of our approach to worship and to life through this Great Prayer.

Notes

1 Frances Young, ' "A Time for Silence". Dare we speak of prayer?' in *Dare we speak of God in public?*, Frances Young (ed.) (Mowbrays, 1995).
2 *Prayer from Alexander to Constantine*. A Critical Anthology, ed. Mark Kiley *et al.* (Routledge: London and New York, 1997).
3 Grant S. White, 'The Recovery of the Great Eucharistic Prayer in the Wesleyan Tradition' (unpublished conference paper).

8 The Fraction and the Shape of the Rite*

David Stancliffe

In the Eucharist there are distinct moments when the two things that God has done for his people – sharing our life and then transforming it – are made visible in the liturgy. These are the moments which focus what God has done for us in sharing our life in his incarnate Word and the transformation of that life by his act of sacrificial love on the Cross. These moments are high points in the liturgy. The first is the proclamation of the Gospel and the second is the breaking of the bread.

But these high points do not stand alone. They are the peaks in the pattern of the whole drama of the eucharistic action which was beginning to take shape at an early stage in the Church's life. By the time that the narrative of Luke's gospel was being formed, the essential shape of the Eucharist, gathered around these two peaks, was clearly being articulated.

Luke uses his account of the way the post-resurrection Church came into being as the context for his exposition, and the narrative in chapter 24 of his gospel begins with the two disciples, trudging back to Emmaus after the momentous events of the previous few days. In spite of Jesus' teaching, they were taken aback by the apparent failure of his mission, and had to be slowly taught again that it is death that leads to life.

The narrative in chapter 24 of Luke's gospel, verses 13 to 35, has four stages. First, the two disciples, who are trailing back home mulling over their disappointment,

*© David Stancliffe 2000

are joined by a stranger who asks them what they are talking about. Prompted by this question, they pour out their dashed expectations, and tell the whole story of what has happened. Second, the stranger now takes the lead, tells them that they are fools not to have made the connections, and gives them a prolonged biblical exegesis so that they can work them out for themselves. But the penny still does not drop. Third, the two disciples reach home and press the stranger, who is clearly going further, to stay. He comes in, sits at table with them, and then takes, blesses and breaks the bread. And suddenly, says St Luke, 'their eyes were opened, and they recognised him, and he vanished from their sight.' Fourth, fired with excitement at the biblical exposition as well as the real presence of the living Lord, they leap up from the table and set out back for Jerusalem at once to tell the others, the despondent, weary journey of the afternoon forgotten.

In that narrative, Luke – how consciously we cannot know – models the pattern of engagement and transformation at the heart of the eucharistic action by which the Church nourishes her life on Christ. And although you can make a simple twofold shape for the Eucharist, of our engagement with Christ in the Liturgy of the Word and our transformation in the Liturgy of the Sacrament, that scarcely does justice to the subtlety of Luke's eucharistic theology, which weaves the memorial of the Last Supper, the real presence now and the pilgrimage pattern of energised discipleship together under the umbrella of the Christ who shares our life, and then changes it.

Taking the four stages of Luke's narrative, we can set them alongside the shape of Order One for the Eucharist in *Common Worship*. The pattern for Order One has four main sections

- *The Gathering*, during which the assembly is constituted by singing together, recalled in penitence to its baptismal status, and prepared to receive the Word of God. This section is summed up in the presidential Collect.
- *The Liturgy of the Word*, during which the assembly engages with the Word, as the story of what God has done in Christ is set alongside the community's experi-

ence, and in the Sermon the implications are teased out for Prayer and action

- *The Liturgy of the Sacrament*, during which the assembly is offered the possibility of transformation as they are incorporated into the one, perfect self-offering of Christ to the Father and receive the body and blood of Christ in faith with thanksgiving
- *The Dismissal*, when the assembly is reminded to put into practice the new life they have received, and are sent out into the community to do it.

This division of the Order One liturgy, articulated clearly by the sectional headings, corresponds closely to the sections in Luke's narrative.

First, the assembly gathers, conscious of being on the way and eager to tell its story – the story of what has happened since we last met. That will include thanksgivings and praise for what has happened as well as some penitential honesty about our failings – although in many people's mind, confession often dominates the opening rites. It is, of course, always easier to look backwards rather than forwards and people can't resist talking about themselves and what they've done instead of what we all might hope to do. That is why the penitential element should be kept firmly in proportion. Perhaps more important is the tuning in, the learning again to attend to God and to each other, to listen to the song of the angels, and to keep an expectant silence, pushing our expectations to the limit. We sometimes forget, like the disciples on the way to Emmaus, to ask about, or even notice the strangers in our midst. And in the middle of all the clutter, we need to remember that the Greeting, silent prayer and a Collect are the bare bones: everything else is padding.

Second, we set the story of who we are, where we are coming from and where we hope to go alongside the story of what God has done for his people. Our ears may be full of the sound of our own voices, and we may think we know the parts of God's story that we would like to hear. But the purpose of a lectionary is for the Church to make sure that we are not just fed a balanced diet of biblical readings, but are confronted with a number of passages we might not choose to hear, because they may challenge our comfortable assumptions. At the heart of this section, as on the walk to Emmaus, are the words of Jesus himself. In the proclamation of the Gospel we are offered a direct encounter with the living Word; that is why we rise, expecting to meet our Lord and Saviour. And it is also why small rituals like taking the Gospel Book round the assembly to be reverenced are important: each person is offered a direct encounter with the incarnate Son. It is the preacher's task to make the encounter a living one, where the incarnate Word is enabled to take root, and radical change can be helped on its way. It is this interaction between Christ and his people and all that they bring with them that should shape the Prayers of the People, a skilful task of sifting, discernment and concise expression traditionally entrusted to that liturgical go-between, the Deacon.

Third, although those disciples were weary, and the penny had not yet dropped, there was still the invitation to step over the threshold with the traditional blessing 'Peace be with you' as the stranger came in. The liturgy, like the work of our redemption, does not end with engagement, with the encounter with the living Word. Actual change, not just the chance to think about it intellectually, is what our salvation offers. So does the eucharistic liturgy. After the Greeting of Peace comes the preparation of the table and the gifts, in which we see – in Augustine's words – 'the mystery of ourselves' upon the altar. In the great Thanksgiving we bless God for his creation and our redemption, praying that we may be made one with him in this foretaste of the heavenly banquet. Then in the most powerful sign in this part of the Eucharist, the bread which has just been consecrated to be the body of Christ is broken. There before our eyes as it was for the disciples at Emmaus is the sign of the death, of the body broken on the cross. That is the moment when their eyes were opened, and the fragments of their memory and experience were tumbled together to produce a life-changing transformation.

As we receive the broken fragment of the host into our hand, we too are offered transformation; a change from being the broken, discordant and fragmentary people that we are into being renewed and whole, members of one single body, ready to act as one. And because we have been caught up into the one perfect sacrifice of Christ to the Father, that reshapes the direction of our lives. We no longer live for ourselves but for him who died and was raised for our salvation.

No wonder then, fourthly, we are impatient to be up and doing. 'Did not our hearts burn within us on the way, while he opened the scriptures to us?' said the disciples. And they were off and away without a second thought. It is tempting to think of the Eucharist as if it were an end in itself, a wonderful pre-echo of a privileged heaven. But there is a rubric at the end 'The ministers and people depart' and it is there for the same reason that the last section of the Eucharist is called The Dismissal, and the whole action is sometimes called the Mass. The root of these words is *missum*, the past participle of the Latin verb which means 'sent', from which our word 'mission' comes. The Church, changed by the celebration of the Eucharist, has been reshaped out of a lot of broken and fragmentary individuals into a united body, ready for action.

The Eucharist offers us the shape for life, for the mission and engagement of the Church. This pattern of engagement and transformation is not something once delivered to the saints and played out daily or weekly in the liturgy as a reminder of a golden, but irretrievably past, age. It is the pattern for our formation in Christ now and always. This means that our participating in it is not only for our salvation, but also for our formation for mission, for our engagement with God's world for its salvation. We have God's people to care for, and engage with directly: a Gift-Aid cheque in an envelope is not the same. We have governments with selfish interests and cheap petrol prices burning holes in the ozone layer with one hand and spending millions on cancer research with the other. We have fear and suspicion, those enemies of peace, walking the land instead of truth and righteousness because what people are most afraid of is meeting each other. The catholic oblation cannot be satisfied with less than a radical programme for catholic action. In other words, to celebrate the

99

Eucharist together and do nothing about feeding the hungry is an act of blasphemy.

That is the shape of the eucharistic celebration from then to now, and I recount it in order to make the peaks visible, and to suggest some ways in which we might make this eucharistic theology visible in the way in which we celebrate.

In order to make the first peak, the incarnation, visible I want first to commend the use of a real Gospel Book. The book, which should contain the full texts of all four gospels, is what is brought into the assembly right at the start. It is the introduction of this icon of the presence of Christ among his people, of the Word made flesh pitching his tent among us – even if he remains unrecognised at this point – which marks the beginning of the rite. This custom was retained in the Presbyterian Church of Scotland, when the Beadle brought in the Bible and placed it on the desk publicly as a signal that the assembly was now in the presence of God. While I know that there is a vogue for gospel books containing the *pericopes* that form the liturgical gospel readings for the three-year cycle of the new lectionary, I think that we need the complete texts of all four gospels. Lectionaries may develop, and anyway, preaching may require an extra verse or two at the beginning or the end to give the context or develop the point. These books – with their beautiful bindings or metalwork book-covers – were among the great treasures of churches in former times – and should be the embodiment of what they contain – God's gift to his people. That is why you cannot read the gospel off a throwaway leaflet.

And it is not just the impression given at the entrance of the ministers. The Gospel Book is carried in style to the place where the Gospel is to be proclaimed, and honoured with lights and incense because we are greeting the living Word made flesh, and we expect that encounter to be life-changing. That is why we rise, and greet the Gospel with alleluias, one of the important chants that the assembly should always sing. It is also the reason why the Gospel is not read, but proclaimed. It may be chanted, or projected in some other way, but it should be distinguished from the other readings.

w/A
Kiss
?

And at the end of the reading, I do not think that it should just be the deacon or whoever has proclaimed the Gospel who should kiss the book; it should be carried round the assembly for people to honour. If we were in the Synagogue and it were the scrolls that were being carried round, the reader would have them hoist on their left shoulder, and people would be reaching out to touch them with the fringes of their prayer-shawls. Making the encounter with the living Word a direct one ought sometimes to offer the possibility of direct physical encounter as the alleluias are repeated.

The second visible peak is the fraction, that utilitarian act by which that whole bread that has been consecrated to be the Body of Christ is broken into pieces so that each person may share in it. But ever since the Emmaus narrative became bedded into the Church's experience, the breaking of the bread has acquired a special significance. That is the moment when memory, sign and present experience were fused in the experience of the disciples, and as Acts (2:46) recalls, it was by the breaking of bread in their homes that the early Christians were distinguished.

For this act to speak as significantly as it should, a minimalist fraction of a small wafer is not enough. I think that the bread needs to be large, and sufficient large breads need to be broken in order that each communicant should receive a broken piece. I know that there is convenience in little individual wafers, but our tradition does not go in for little individual communion cups, and I cannot think that the small wafers are right either. The significant sign is broken bread. Breaking may take some time, but the presiding celebrant may be assisted by others if there are many communicants. The Agnus Dei should be repeated until all the bread is broken and the chalices filled. For the principle that says there should be one large dish or plate on the altar also says that there should be one large chalice.

In the classical world, a *calix* was a large mixing bowl, frequently with handles and a small lip for pouring out. At large celebrations, the focus on one bread and one cup is best preserved by having only two vessels on the altar, rather than a forest of smaller cups and ciboria. Those who are assisting in the distribution bring the vessels from which they are going to distribute up to the altar with them as the Agnus Dei begins, and the presiding celebrant puts broken bread into some while the deacon pours the consecrated wine out of the one *calix*. The group around the altar then breaks outwards to the places where the distribution of communion takes place, and so writes the sign large.

This is an alternative to the practice of assistants or concelebrants bringing a number of smaller charged vessels into the assembly as the altar is prepared, and holding them in their hands during the Eucharistic prayer. That pattern too can be visually effective as those vessels are raised in time with the presiding celebrant's actions during the prayer – especially when they are all raised together during the doxology. The group that has surrounded the altar then breaks outwards as the bread is broken.

Whichever of these patterns seems appropriate in each context offers a visual focus to the sign that holds before us the cross with its broken body, the sign of our redemption.

I add these comments on good practice to my theological reflection on the Lukan shape of our eucharistic offering in order to draw out what the Liturgical Commission in its recent writings has called the 'deep structures of the Liturgy'.

The deep structures of the liturgy run at a number of different levels. First, there is the structure or shape revealed by the historic practice and developing tradition of the Church. The evolution of this pattern can be traced from the early days of the Church. It is grounded in the experience recorded in the New Testament of those disciples who had been there at the Last Supper, witnessed the Crucifixion and then had met the risen Christ in the Breaking of the bread. Liturgical archaeologists – of whom I would not claim to be one – are at home in this world, charting the doctrinal shifts in eucharistic theology and peeling away the later mediaeval accretions with which popular piety and clerical devotion have overlaid the original in an attempt to unearth the pure form of the original rite of the undivided Church. In this search for an ideal, the basic skeleton is laid bare, and the eucharistic rite of most of the western Churches now bear a remarkable similarity. The shape – the skeletal structure – of Order One is identical to that in the Roman Sacramentary, and to the orders in the Lutheran and Presbyterian Churches worldwide.

A second deep structure is that which the theological reflections in this chapter have already revealed. There is a theological shape as well as a liturgical shape to the rites not only of Eucharist, but of baptism, marriage, funerals and of patterns like vigil rites. At their heart, rites are vehicles of transformation, means of catching a worshipping assembly into the divine life of the Holy Trinity. Worship gives space for the Spirit to move within the pattern of ordered activity, and takes seriously God's engagement with his people. All worship worthy of the name models that pattern of engagement and transformation which is at the heart of what God has done for us in Christ in incarnation and redemption. Encounter with the divine Word is never fruitless: 'it will not return to me empty', as Isaiah says (55:11). There is always some change, some movement as we are caught up into 'the upward call of God in Christ Jesus' (Phil. 3:14) and drawn into the one, perfect self-offering of Christ to the Father.

Liturgies that do not offer an opportunity to rehearse this pattern of encounter and change, of meeting that leads to growth and development, become static and lose their shape and direction. In addition, they fail to engage with our deepest longings and so remain at the level of spectacle or entertainment. Worshippers become spectators, and the performance is conducted before them. This is why it is important for those who devise worship to understand the drama of our salvation, which may be laid out as in the great Passiontide hymn of *Venatius Fortunatus* 'Sing my tongue the glorious battle', or in Bishop Benson's Festival of Nine Lesson and Carols, or in the Baptismal Liturgy of Easter. Whichever of these you choose, the underlying sense of movement is the same as we are caught into the continuing pattern of the divine activity.

But third, this is not just a theological pattern; it is also one that is deeply tuned to human experience. The deep structures of human life and longing which the social anthropologists have revealed uncover a pattern of movement and growth which liturgies need to attend to if they

103

are to ring true to human experience and engage with it. Our knowledge of the processes of loss, anger, letting go and bereavement have helped us shape funeral rites – even when the elements have to be compacted into one short act of worship – which are not only rooted in a theology of the movement from death to resurrection, but take account of the stages through which the processes of death and bereavement take us. Many rites have this 'staged' pattern. The initiation rites are an obvious example, which again need to recapitulate briefly the long process of conversion, of being drawn into a community, engaging with its story, finding the security to let yourself be challenged about your past and future, and so coming to the baptismal waters at a point in the process when the journey to that point is equalled by the lifetime's pilgrimage which stretches ahead. Baptism is discovered to be about Spirit-led growth towards maturity within the life of the community of faith as much as a moment of decision which is mine and mine alone. This deep structure is as important as its liturgical and theological counterparts, and is what enables liturgies to have their power and direction.

The other factor I have briefly mentioned in this reflection on the twin peaks in the eucharistic liturgy of Gospel proclamation and the Breaking of the Bread is order. The liturgy exhibits a pattern and order which reflects something of the divine plan for the Cosmos. That order is expressed in how different elements of the liturgy and different gifts within the assembly are related to one another within the whole offering of worship. As individuals, our story is known and valued, but we find our identity before God within a continuing pattern of evolving response to his gift to us. We do not stand alone, and more importantly, we do not sing from our own, individual hymn-sheet.

 The human activity that has always been at the centre of worship is singing. In the Orthodox tradition there is no such thing as a 'Low Mass'. You either celebrate the liturgy solemnly or not at all, and something of this tradition is visible in the charismatic movement where singing a carefully constructed sequence of songs together is known as 'a time of worship'. And no one who has been to Africa would deny the inescapable power of singing to take you out of yourself.

I believe that this is really important for the catholic tradition to grasp. Singing together in parts models that unity which is a rich harmony, rather than the narrow uniformity of a flat unison. That is why I want to give you an experience of singing together which we can all take part in, using music which we can sing together with confidence after a few moments rehearsal.

MUSIC for EUCHARISTIC PRAYER G   John Harper

. . . we may find a voice to sing your praise: Ho-ly, ho-ly, ho - ly Lord,

God of power and might,   hea-ven and earth are full of your glo-ry.

Ho-san-na in the high - est.   Bles - sed is   he who comes in the

name of the Lord.   Ho - san - na   in the high - est.

Christ has died: Christ is risen: Christ will come a - gain.

Blessing and honour and glo-ry and power be yours for e-ver and e-ver, A - men.

9 The Post Communion Prayer – Living Sacrifice*

Joseph P. Cassidy

I have been asked to consider the Post Communion Prayer, in which we offer our souls and bodies as a living sacrifice, and in which we pray to be sent in the power of the Spirit into our world. So I first want to say something about our sense of being sent, our sense of knowing or hoping that what we have just celebrated in the Eucharist will make a real difference in our lives.

I was also asked to do this with an eye to my own field of ethics, seeing an ethical dimension to our eucharistic response, so the second thing I want to do is consider whether the way we live our lives, the way we make our decisions, the strategies we collectively adopt – whether and how these can be centred on the Eucharist.

And thirdly (given that this was delivered as the final address) I was asked to try to discern where the Spirit had been moving during the conference as we prepared for our final conference Eucharist.

Earlier in this book – as in the conference – Bill Countryman and Rowan Williams have spoken of the kind of in-between space we find ourselves in, emphasising our groaning and our reaching out, and noting how mystery sometimes gets confused with ambiguity, or how we fly from mystery into the idolatry of a forced clarity. I would like to suggest that the Eucharist itself, and our reaction to the event of receiving Communion alongside one another

*© Joseph P. Cassidy 2000

– are also marked by mystery, by incompleteness, by an urge to continue to reach for what seems elusive. The Eucharist can itself be prey to the idolatry of forced clarity.

Have you noticed how strange it is that, though we believe in Jesus' real presence, though we believe that through the Eucharist we encounter not just a bit of Jesus but the whole reality of Jesus Christ, nevertheless, this encounter is not the Second Coming?

Do you find it strange that 'every time we eat this bread and drink this cup, we proclaim the Lord's death *until he comes*'? Is that not what he is supposed to be doing? Is he not, in some way or other, precisely *coming* to us, uniting us to one another and to himself in a real communion? That is why, as David Stancliffe has written, he is properly to be found precisely in broken bread, in the actual sharing of broken bread. When we eat broken bread and drink wine outpoured, we *are* encountering the real Jesus who offers himself to us completely and unreservedly, who becomes closer to us than closeness itself, and who is none-theless '*yet to come*'.

It would be a good example of the idolatry of forced clarity were I to pretend for one moment that I could explain such a mystery, even though others have tried to do so in terms of distinguishing between a spiritual pres-ence and a local presence, or a personal presence and a corporeal presence. Frankly, I remain suspicious of all such explanations. The distinctions are variously made to pre-clude any mingling of the two natures or any separation of the two natures of Christ. However, in trying to avoid one trap, the explanations seem inevitably to fall into the other trap. I do not particularly want to split Jesus into two, to drive a wedge between his humanity and divinity.

What I do want to do is suggest that there is something profoundly right-headed, right-spirited, and right-hearted about our experience that when we come closest to Jesus he does not let us cling to him; he really does elude our complete grasp. I want to emphasise that he prevents us from clutching on to him not by absenting himself, but *by commissioning us, by sending us out*. This should not surprise us: at the end of Matthew's gospel, Jesus briefly appears to the women and sends them to tell the disciples to go and meet him in Galilee. A few lines later at the account of the Ascension, we read of a commissioning. The same sort of thing can be found in the longer ending of Mark, and it is implicit in the other gospels as well. Those appearance narratives are all about a kind of 'real presence' of Jesus, but the Evangelists were at pains to describe an elusive more-real-than-real type of presence that destroys all our categories of what is real. The all-too-real presence calls us beyond the present.

Teresa of Avila

I want now to make what may seem like a surprising excursus into the spirituality of Teresa of Avila. I do so to make the point that this experience of communion with Jesus, who does not let us cling to him by commissioning us, is characteristic not just of what we may experience in the Eucharist, but also of the flow of one of the more compelling spiritual traditions in the western Church.[1]

Those of you who know something of the spirituality of Teresa of Avila or of John of the Cross would know that the whole spiritual struggle can be expressed in terms of our trying to contain God. And oddly, God lets us try. God even meets us where we are. That is why in the initial months and years of prayer, God encourages us by letting us experience delight in the divine presence, by letting us feel as though we have been swept deliriously off our feet. Yet, in time, as the relationship matures, and as these palpable consolations either disappear or they lose their attraction, we are urged to love God for God's sake alone, and not for the delight that often accompanies our getting a bit closer to God. Now and then, we may begin to feel all this very acutely, as the Spirit increases our desire for God, while at the same time God becomes exquisitely distant. The person praying almost explodes with desire and at the same time implodes with the tight concentration of unfulfilled love. You think you are going to die from desire, or as St Teresa described it in her third poem, you feel impaled on the dart of love. And as you sit and indeed as you live with that wound of love, as that all-consuming desire becomes strangely familiar, you actually start identifying with the desire. You become the desire. The desire is your life. Vestigial compulsion then gives way to a strange sense of freedom, as you, the desire, all at once realise that you cannot cause God, that God really is pure, utter graciousness. And, when you have given up, when you are tired of beating your soul against the wall, when for the umpteenth time you decide to let God be God, God comes to you, though not quite in the way you might have expected. In a very short time, gone is the rapture; gone are the most intense interrupting consolations; gone are any desires to possess or even to be possessed (in a demonic sense) by the beloved (p. 342). Instead you discover, perhaps for the first time, and this is the point of all this – *you discover real apostolicity.* Your passion changes from desiring God's presence, to becoming more and more in sync with the inner life of the Trinity, where the Father eternally offers life to the Son, and where the Son, as a living sacrifice, eternally offers it back to the Father, and where the life offered and re-offered is so utterly personal that the exchange eternally constitutes another person, the Holy Spirit – and perhaps even your innermost self (p. 332).

Well, the surprise in Teresa of Avila's prayer is that this exquisite familiarity with God, this spiritual marriage, this being united to the living sacrifice which is the life of the Trinity – this is no form of absorption (p. 332). When you have been through the dark night of the soul and the dark night of the spirit (as John describes them), when you have moved from betrothal to spiritual marriage (as Teresa describes it), when God has so moulded you that God invites you to experience the Trinity (the seventh mansion), the result is not rapture nor ecstasy. Those experiences belong to an earlier phase. No, the epitome of the contemplative life, indeed of the whole Christian life, for Teresa at least, is a type of peace, a type of assurance that results in a type of freedom, which then enables you solely to 'be about the Lord's business' (p. 339). It is the freedom to be sent. It is discipleship with an all-too-human Jesus (p. 334) who invites us to be filled with the very same Spirit who filled him. To put words into Teresa's mouth, this call to service requires us to dedicate our entire selves – souls and bodies – to become one living sacrifice, not in an out-of-this world sense (p. 347), but through our very incarnate and often simple living and working in the world. The epitome of Teresa's prayer life is thus precisely a type of commissioning. It is not an arriving, but a beginning. Teresa tells us that, at this point in her spiritual journey, in what she described as the seventh mansion, she was able to tell the difference between hearing and believing the core message of the Gospel as though for the first time (p. 332). She had not arrived; she was just about to begin.

I have belaboured this Teresian excursus on purpose. I want to acknowledge our catholic tradition's taste for the contemplative, for the mystical, for the possibility of an intimate union with God, because it is a huge part of what we hope for in the Eucharist. At the same time, this sort of expectation points to a problem with the way we pray that post-communion prayer.

I mean, don't you sometimes find it intrusive? Don't you find the change of gears a bit rough? Don't you find yourself trying to be present to what-you've-just-said-Amen-to in communion, only to be interrupted by the priest who wants to get on with it? So much so that when he or she says 'Let us pray' after communion, part of you wants to say, 'I would, if you'd only shut up.'

There's something in us that expects communion to be a type of momentary mystical communion, a foretaste of heaven, an encounter between heaven and earth, maybe even a mini second-coming – a sneak preview. Now, I do not want to undermine any of that, because that is all part of the wonderful expectations we legitimately bring to the Eucharist. Nevertheless, the rhythm of the Eucharist takes us somewhere else; and the eucharistic rhythm is, as I said, strikingly akin to the rhythm of contemplative prayer. The end is but a beginning, and the communion is a communion with our God who, like it or not, is busy, bending over backwards, trying to save our world.

But we do resist it, don't we? Isn't it funny that, all over the world, after communion, after the commissioning that occurs with the blessing, all Anglicans kneel down again? It is as though we were trying to hang on to that intimacy. It would be a bit like those women in Matthew's gospel, after being sent by Jesus, saying to Jesus, 'Hang on, hang on, we'll go when we're ready. We just want to wait a while to savour the moment.' With due deference to Bill Countryman, it sounds vaguely like one of those Californian jokes; or, if not that, at least reminiscent of the Transfiguration temptation to build a tent. (I remember when I first began going to Anglican Eucharists, beginning to follow the procession out of church, and then sheepishly kneeling down again, trying to figure out what everyone was waiting for, what the cue was to tell us when an appropriately pious length of time had passed before I could get up.)

I want to change gears again; but before I do, I would like just to highlight the key points I have been trying to make. The real Jesus we encounter in the Eucharist, in the Gospel, in the community, in the sharing of broken bread – this real Jesus is never someone we can possess. He remains the one who is to come. And this is not just a quality of the Eucharist. It conforms to what we find in at least one of our major western spiritualities. While we may want to be absorbed into Jesus through communion, and though we may want to cling to him when we do encounter him, he is more likely to commission us. The Post Communion Prayer quite properly urges us on, whether we like it or not.

Christian Ethics

I shall come back to all of this later, but I would like, as expected, to address the ethics side of things. First, though, I want to assure you that the link between the Post Communion Prayer and ethics is not being unnaturally forced. In Romans 12:1, the source of our Post Communion Prayer, Paul says,

> (1) I appeal to you therefore, brethren, by the mercies of God, to present your bodies as a living sacrifice, holy and acceptable to God, which is your spiritual worship.

Then he says,

> (2) Do not be conformed to this world, but be transformed by

111

the renewal of your mind, that you may prove what is the
will of God, what is good and acceptable and perfect.

In this second part of my address, I want to speak of this
transformation, this renewal that will allow us to discover
the will of God, and so discover 'what is good'. In doing
so, you will hear echoes of Bishop David Stancliffe's mini-
creed: God shares our life, and God changes it.

Before I do so, I want to say that it may look as though
I am disagreeing with a line in Professor Young's chapter
when she reminded us that the Eucharist is not about
emotions. I want to agree that the Eucharist is not about the
emotions that we happen to have. I want to agree that we
do not celebrate the Eucharist because, narcissistically,
we want to squeeze a particular feeling out of it. I want to
agree that there is something 'objective' going on. I even
want to agree that, if emotions are part of what is going
on, it is perhaps Jesus' emotions, Jesus' intentions, Jesus'
desires that are paramount, not ours.

But I do not want to let go of the emotions, because I
want to look at something that is stirring in ethics these
days and which may help us to appreciate the need really
to emphasise this post-communion commissioning, the
need to invest it with as much feeling and passion as we
can muster. First a bit of a story. It is a stolen story but, as
you will see, it is a story that gives us a clue about what
happens when God shares our life, and what happens
when God changes us.

A few years ago, because of a tip from a BBC radio
programme, I read a book entitled *Descartes' Error* by
Antonio Damasio.[2] He tells the true story of Phineas Gage,
who had been a railway engineer in the Green Mountains
of Vermont at the turn of the century. Phineas Gage was
responsible for ensuring that dynamite charges had been
set properly. The crew would drill a hole in the stone,
dynamite would be placed in the hole, a fuse would be
added and then sand would be placed on top to ensure
the explosion was directed through the rock instead of
shooting out of the hole. Phineas' job was to stick a rod
into each hole to ensure that the sand had been properly
tamped down before the dynamite was ignited. Well, one

day, he poked the metal rod into one of these holes, only to find that there was no sand. The metal rod came into direct contact with stone. There was a spark, the dynamite exploded, and the rod shot up out of the hole and pierced Phineas' left cheek, emerging through the top of his skull.

Well, Phineas survived. Not only did he survive, but also he never lost consciousness. Over the years, however, he and others noticed that he could do everything except organise his life. In fact, his inability to organise his life was so tragic and extreme that he could not hold down a job, and he ended up a drifter.

After he died, his skull was preserved, and Antonio Damasio, a neurologist, became interested in his injury, especially because Damasio had been studying people who had suffered from brain tumours in exactly the same part of the brain as Phineas Gage.

He studied this group of people, and he found that they had all had this same problem with organising their lives. He assumed, quite naturally, that their reasoning powers were somehow impaired. However, after batteries of tests, the subjects of his study showed that they were actually excellent at thinking. They were even excellent at solving moral dilemmas and reasoning about choices in life. The problem was that, in day-to-day life, they were incapable of making good decisions.

Then a pattern began to emerge. Having realised that there was nothing at all wrong with their reasoning, with their rational, conceptual or abstract abilities, there was nonetheless one striking difference about people with this brain injury: they were emotionally detached. They could not engage emotionally with life. They did not have moods, *per se*, and when confronted with a decision, they were unusually capable of approaching decisions dispassion- ately, with cool objectivity. But there was no emotional engagement.

Damasio's little book takes on René Descartes, the father of rationalism. It is this rationalism that Damasio calls, 'Descartes' Error'. Damasio realised that, without feelings, without emotions, we cannot make decisions. Moreover, to the extent that we have driven a wedge between our various abilities to reason and to feel – to that extent we have made good decisions impossible.

Not a very earth-shattering discovery, though, is it? Any one of us could have made the same discovery by looking at how we ourselves operate. In fact, many years earlier, the Canadian philosopher–theologian Bernard Lonergan insisted that 'feelings, not our intellects, apprehend values'. Be that as it may, can you imagine life without feelings? Can you imagine what it would be like to have no desires? Though you could perhaps make decisions, why would you bother? How would you know which decisions to make? Ethicists for generations have been paranoid about giving feelings any sort of role in decision-making because we were convinced that feelings would undermine the reasonableness of the good, and it was only on the basis of reasonableness that we could urge each other, or so we thought, to act ethically. Descartes did it. Hume sort of did it, though he realised that passions and action were linked. Kant most famously did it by insisting that ethical obligation is rational obligation, and that the influence of the passions makes decisions selfish.

What Damasio called for is an appreciation that human decision-making must be integrated. Like it or not, human decision-making is the art of weaving together our bodily, our emotional, our intellectual, and, I would add, our spiritual ways of being.

Another story, if I may. In 1971, my ethics lecturer told us a story that is still with me today. He said, suppose you are a father or mother, and your child has just fallen into the Niagara River and she is hurtling towards Niagara Falls. Imagine time stopping for a moment to allow you to figure out how to respond. The seminar group discussed with him the various possibilities: one of us suggested that we would jump in and try to save the child, but he assured us that the child could not be saved; you might just be able to catch up with her, but the current was too strong to save her. And so we discussed whether jumping in and trying anyway would be suicide, whether it was better for one life to be lost than for two, and so on. We were trying to be very reasonable. In the end, we decided that we ought not to do anything, though lots of us said that, had time not stood still, we would probably, and rather irrationally, jump in anyway. We asked him what he would do, and he said he would jump in not to try to save her, but to hold on to her as she went to her death.

I am still moved by that little exercise, especially now that I have children of my own. I am moved not because that is so obviously the best thing to do: what moves me is the love that could imagine such an option. I am moved also by what was then and what still is a strangely different way of making a decision. You will notice that feelings are paramount. You will notice that your heart was engaged. You will even notice that the hint of irrationality is part of what makes the story compelling. *You know, what we remember in the Eucharist is compelling in exactly the same way.*

Ethics and the Post Communion Prayer

Well, that is a long way of making a very simple point: no feelings – no decisions. With that point made, it is probably time that I begin to show how I think the two parts of this chapter belong together. If the Post Communion Prayer is about commissioning us; if one of the things we expect from the Eucharist is a way *into* our world; if, as Rowan Williams suggests, what we are really talking about is conversion – witnessing to the powerful possibility of conversion; then we ought to expect the Eucharist to change the way we make decisions, to change the kinds of decisions we make. Again, as several other contributors have stated, we ought to expect faith to make a difference; we ought to expect our preaching to make a difference; we ought to expect our encountering God to make a difference: God meets us, and God changes us. *Well, if Damasio is right, nothing will happen unless we are engaged emotionally.* Understanding theological truth cannot move you. Saying 'Lord, Lord' cannot save you. Believing that the Lord is present in this way or that way in communion will, on its own, make no difference.

Again, none of this should surprise us. I recall working in a maximum-security psychiatric prison for four months. One of my more vivid recollections was meeting an inmate who was full of rage, who was physically dangerous. Talk about feelings, talk about feelings affecting decisions, talk about fear as I met this chap in his confined cell! But I can also recall something more frightening, and that was meeting an inmate whose emotional life had been shut down chemically, by mood-stabilising drugs, by tranquillisers. I should say that I fully appreciate that this is sometimes medically necessary; but that encounter *really* scared me; and, to be honest, I felt something almost demonic in the emotional disengagement.

The thing about feelings, about desires, is that they do not come alone. We are a bundle of feelings. In addition, one of the more interesting things about our feelings is that they emerge in terms of a scale of preferences, in terms of a scale of passions.[3] Moreover, this scale is not just a matter of which one feels the strongest, or which ones are closest to the surface of consciousness. No. Each of us has an affective scale of importance, a scale of commitment, as it were. That is why, without the emotional components, good choices could simply not be made. That unfortunate group of people with brain dysfunction could not prefer. They *could* tell which decisions were better, but they could not emotionally prefer the better. It is weird: imagine knowing that chocolate cake is better than vanilla cake but not being able to *feel* preference, not being able to desire the desirable, not being able to prefer the preferable?

Again, an interesting thing about this scale of preferences, or as we say in ethics, this scale of values, is that, if your brain *is* functioning more or less properly, you have *got* a scale of values whether you like it or not. (That is part of the fun of exposing ethical relativists: you can always show them that they have strong preferences after all.) But the point I want to make is that, if we want to change our decision-making, if we want the Eucharist to make a difference, if we want God to change us, if we are willing to be commissioned to make a difference, we are going to have to allow God to change the way we scale our values, to change our preferences, to change our feelings, to change our felt-priorities. That is what change is all about. That is what happens when hearts of stone are changed into hearts of flesh. If faith is about believing that God can convert us, turn us around, and forgive us in such a way that we truly are changed, then God is going to do a lot of work in and through our feelings.

I believe this means that authentic prayer, and that includes authentic liturgical prayer, is very likely to be much more *affective* than intellectual – and it does not matter what sort of Myers–Briggs or Enneagram type you are. Phineas Gage's brain proved that.

Again, none of this is entirely novel. It is summed up in Psalm 39: 'Taste and see that the Lord is good.' You could pray that one line of Scripture for the rest of your lives and not exhaust it. Or by St Ignatius of Loyola, when, in his second introductory observation to his *Spiritual Exercises*, he insists 'that it is not much knowledge that fills and satisfies the soul, but the intimate understanding and relish of the truth.' Or by my Old Testament Professor, Professor R. A. F. MacKenzie, who read the first account of creation in Genesis, concluding each day with, 'And God saw that it was . . .' – smacking his lips before saying, 'good'. It felt as though he had wanted to say 'finger-licking good' and maybe he should have done. The point he wanted to make, and he did so brilliantly, was that God was not making a moral judgement about creation. God was expressing God's delight with the creation.

Let me spell out some of the very simple and obvious repercussions of taking feelings on board.

Beginning with ethics, I wonder whether we need to rediscover conscience. Despite what I have been teaching for the last 20 years, conscience is not just the ability to make correct moral judgements. Judgements are normally *intellectual* acts. What characterises moral judgement is not just our stating a moral fact about something, but our staking a claim that something is really preferable to something else. The older way of talking about conscience in terms of feeling tensions within, feeling a disturbance, feeling an upset in our scale of values, feeling something as being out of step, or feeling the sting of conscience – there's something very right about all that, after all. Similarly, when we relish the good, when we feel our affections pointing us towards a particular decision, when there is a consonance within us, a sense of peace even in the face of tragic choices, then we need to learn to trust those affect-

117

laden interior senses.[4] For too long we have separated discernment of spirits from moral deliberation. To that extent, we have separated the good from the desirable. We identify the good, but we do not actually prefer it. In that one insight is a whole agenda for a profound change in the way we approach moral education and preaching on ethical matters. There is also an agenda for marrying spirituality and ethics, for linking contemplation and action, and for regaining some ethical respectability for the Churches. Unless we are enthralled by the good, we shall not choose the good. The catholic tradition, with its confidence in the goodness of God's creation, with its appreciation of the contemplative, with its expectation that God really can address our very soul, with its ultimate focus on love as the ultimate divine strategy – this tradition has much to say to our world today.

Closely related, and perhaps even more fundamental, is the need (once again) to rediscover the Holy Spirit. If all that I have said about feelings and emotions is true, then we need to focus much more on our belief in the indwelling of the Holy Spirit. If the Holy Spirit is groaning within us; if the Holy Spirit is loving the Father and the Son and is being loved by the Father and Son with such a love that it binds the distinct persons of the Trinity together; if that supreme power is actually within us, constituting us, sourcing and re-sourcing us; and if any of that is palpable – if we can feel anything of that at all – then the keys to the kingdom of God are truly within us.

By that I mean that, if our feelings are so very crucial, and if the Holy Spirit is present to us in terms of her pure groaning for God, then, if we are in touch with the whole range of our feelings, we ought to expect to be able to sense when our desires are out of sync with divine desire; we ought to expect to be able to tell, if we would but listen, when our desires are at one with divine desire. That will be the only sure ground for our preferring. Is it too much to suggest that, were we to develop the wisdom to read what the Spirit does in people's hearts, then we would better understand the twin processes of discernment and reception that we in the Anglican Communion so pointedly need at this point in our history?

And if we need proof of just how pivotal this is, we need only look to Jesus' baptism. What happened at the baptism? What difference did that make to Jesus? How was Jesus changed? Well (and this is especially apparent in Luke's account), the baptism had all the hallmarks of a conversion experience, didn't it? And the content seems to have been very affective. In his heart of hearts (if we follow Mark and Luke), Jesus hears God say 'I love you. I'm pleased with you.' That affective experience was so powerful that he struggled for the proverbial forty days and forty nights, having his scale of values painfully redirected, as he agonisingly discerned what it could possibly mean to be so loved by God. He emerged from the wilderness with a sense of having been commissioned; of having his priorities, his preferences, transformed; with a sense of having been anointed to proclaim good news to the poor. He spoke with authority because his scale of values was authentic. And he challenged people to do likewise. Remember, 'What would it profit someone if he or she were to gain the whole world and yet lose his or her life?' Or remember poor Martha who worried about so many things, when only one thing was important. Or remember the many different ways he tried to get across the simple but transforming point that God is so trustworthy that you can dare to love one another, even your enemy, no matter what happens. God is that trustworthy.

If we need to pay more attention to feelings, we need also to realise the power of the imagination, for they almost always walk hand-in-hand. For too long we have dismissed imagination as fantasy, and fantasy as suspect, because it was tantamount to self-deception (which explains why some of our co-religionists remain highly sceptical of using the imagination in prayer). However, imagination is really the power to render reality conceivable. We cannot think without some exercise of our imagination. We cannot make choices without imagining options. We cannot make good choices *without noticing how we feel as we imagine possible choices*. And, fortunately, that is possible because our imaginations are evocative. They are emotionally evocative. Say to someone that Tom has the disease on page 12 of a medical manual, and he or she will give

119

you a puzzled look. But describe the disease, engage the imagination, and all of a sudden compassion has a toehold.[5]

So we need to use *our* imaginations, and we need to appeal to people's hearts via *their* imaginations in our preaching, in our teaching, and not just from the pulpit. We need to see liturgy as an especially sacred exercise of imagination. And because we don't want to be manipulative, we need to be incredibly careful not to tell people what they *ought* to feel in liturgy, but instead be willing to give feelings and imagination some open space. We do this chiefly by using symbols, gestures, ritual, and allowing time for silence. Just as feelings are expressed symbolically in our dreams, so our religious symbol systems *generate* feelings. To use the stony heart image again, God has willingly changed hearts of stone to hearts of flesh through liturgical imagination for thousands of years. The Trinity is very good at it.

I want now to suggest that we ought to expect the Eucharist to make a difference in our lives at an affective level, perhaps even *primarily* at an affective level. It seems to me that the catholic tradition has always understood and expected this, and that is why we have invested so much in terms of gesture, ritual, symbol, music, art and architecture, realising their evocative power. We have realised that liturgy is an affair of the heart, that doxology, in which we cry out the glory of God, is a fundament of right action. Today many of us realise that our liturgy needs to be much more embodied than it has been. We sweat blood over the words, but we all know that it is so much more than words. And because feelings are not just manufactured and located in our brains, we appreciate that they affect our entire bodies, they affect our energy levels, they get expressed in terms of facial expressions, in how we carry ourselves, in the stiffness or naturalness of our gestures, in the warmth of the look in our eyes. There is something very right-headed and right-hearted about the need to become so much more aware of how authentic, how affectively evocative our liturgical movements and gestures are, and not expect words to do all the communicative work.[6]

In the end, if we are not affectively engaged by the

liturgy, then both the post communion commissioning and the dismissal will ring hollow. If we are not affectively engaged by our being commissioned, then we shall not actually be able *to prefer* God's will, and all our ethical deliberations will have been wasted. That is why we need to be open not only to the possibility of religious conversion, but also to the possibility of *affective conversion*. The Post Communion Prayer, when prayed from the heart, can be a good litmus test of whether we have said 'Amen' to the real Jesus.

Notes

1 The page references are to *The Complete Works of Saint Teresa of Jesus*, vol. II, trans. E. Allison Peers (London: Sheed and Ward, 1946).

2 See Antonio Damasio, *Descartes' Error* (New York: Avon, 1994). Here I am liberally paraphrasing Timothy O'Connell's apt shorthand description of Damasio's story. See O'Connell, *Making Disciples* (New York: Crossroad, 1998), pp. 65ff.

3 Here I am pointing again to the work of Bernard Lonergan and to Robert Doran. See Bernard Lonergan, *Method in Theology* (London: Darton, Longman and Todd, 1972), p. 50; and Robert Doran, *Theology and the Dialectics of History* (Toronto: University of Toronto Press, 1990).

4 This feeling of peace is sometimes called *complacentia*, especially in Aquinas.

5 We need especially to use our imaginations when we read Scripture. The evangelists would drop dead (again) if they thought that we'd attempt to read the gospels without allowing those stories to come alive. They would have considered themselves failed storytellers if we did not embellish the stories with all those little imaginary details that make a story really juicy. They would have scratched their heads in disbelief if they thought that their reconstruction of Jesus' life did not make him imaginable, which is to say 'real'. They tried to tell us the story that explains why they had fallen in love with Jesus, and you cannot read a love story with your heart folded away in your back pocket.

6 Nor should we throw stones. The Reformation tradition might have been mistaken to eschew so much of our ritual past, but they were entirely right to celebrate the evocativeness of Scripture, and to expect or even require the sermon to move us.

10 The Dismissal*

Stephen Cottrell

*Sermon at the final Eucharist of the
Living the Eucharist Conference of Affirming Catholicism,
preached at St Oswald's, Durham, 17 September 2000*

> *Oh sing a new song to the Lord!*
> Psalm 149:1

I think it was Mae West who said, 'If you've got it, flaunt it!' This seems to me to be a good text for catholic Christians. The trouble is, however, although we've got it – an understanding of Christianity that is wonderful good news for the world – we rarely flaunt it.

Some years ago I was teaching about evangelism, emphasising that as we seek to share the Gospel with those outside the Church we need to meet people where they are, on their own territory, and accompany them on a journey into faith. After I had spoken a very earnest young clergyman came up to me, worried by what I had been saying, and said that surely we had to tell people the bad news first.

Now I have often suspected that this is what some Christians believe, but I had never before heard it put quite so plainly. The bad news is that you are a sinner who must repent or else you are going to rot in hell for eternity.

I simply reminded him that the word gospel means *good news*. God comes to meet us in Christ, and the first word of the Gospel is good. We have a God who loves us. The Scriptures say that from the first moment of our being, when we were just a couple of cells dividing into life in

*© Stephen Cottrell 2000

the flood tide of our mother's womb, we were known and loved by God. The Gospel is first of all about a God who loves us unconditionally. There is nothing we can do to stop God loving us.

And it is new – probing and challenging and expanding our understanding of ourselves, of our universe and of this mysterious and beautiful God that we know through Jesus Christ.

Please don't misunderstand me, this is not to say that sin is not real and forgiveness unnecessary: the Cross of Jesus Christ is still at the heart of our faith, bringing reconciliation to the world. It is just that we need to understand the Cross and the call to repentance within the context of God's endless loving and his desire for us to be the people he created us to be. It is the vision of what we can become in Christ that is the call of the Gospel.

Last year I led a mission to St John's, South Bank, a lovely parish close to Middlesbrough. Each evening we went to one of the local pubs. Now South Bank is a very poor estate, and these were very seedy pubs. But, after initial suspicion (it is not every day that four priests and two religious come into your pub!) we were made welcome, discovering among the locals a great love for karaoke. We happily joined in.

On the last evening of the mission, after we had finished singing (I think it was Gloria Gaynor's 'I will survive' – an Anglo-Catholic classic!) the DJ asked, over the microphone through the PA system, 'Why did we sing songs that nobody knows?'

I thought he meant why were we always choosing songs on the karaoke by Abba and Donna Summer. I started to explain our choice of music – again, over the PA so the whole pub was listening – when he interrupted me. No, he didn't mean here in the pub, but in the church. Why, in the church, did we sing songs that nobody knows?

And I didn't have an answer. He was right. The world does not understand the songs we are singing.

Our response is either to sing louder, in a vain attempt to drown out the songs of the world. Or to dress up a never changing Gospel in some new cultural clothes, i.e. we'll stick with the same words, but learn some new tunes.

123

What we need to realise is that the words themselves may need changing. Of course in one sense the Gospel does never change. But in another it is constantly changing, readjusting to new circumstances, but also being rediscovered in fresh and challenging ways as we engage with the world around us. The cultural adaptability of the Christian faith is one of the main reasons it has continued to flourish. Because of the Incarnation the 'enfleshing' of Christian faith in individuals and in cultures is, quite literally, in our DNA. We need, then, to stop thinking of the Gospel as a package deal, all neatly sown up, and think of it instead as a multi-faceted jewel. And there are new faces to discover.

And this is particularly relevant for Affirming Catholicism. Between the fundamentalism of Catholic and Protestant alike, who would have it that the Gospel is a closed book, and a certain kind of liberal who claim it is a blank page, we bear witness to a Gospel that is a story being continued. We believe that as we live and share the Gospel as part of a living tradition, so we shall find new things to say, new faces of Christ to adore, new songs to sing.

We place ourselves in the flow of God's sending love to the world, wanting the story of what God has done in Jesus Christ to be incarnate in our lives. We test our discoveries against the Scriptures and the tradition, not inventing the Gospel but discovering what has always been there, but has not yet been seen.

We need to be more upbeat about what we have to offer. We have a Gospel for the world. Too often we let the rest of the Church set the agenda, and too often our aim seems to be little more than wanting our place in the Church. Yet we live in a world that is beginning to think that before you can become a Christian you also have to be a homophobic patriarch. We have something else to offer. No, we can't always sing songs that everyone will always understand because we can never contain God within the confines of our own understanding, but we do have some good news! – a Gospel that celebrates diversity and that is searching for authentic community and true humanity. We might call this a new song. The song that God has given Affirming

Catholicism to sing. A song that can renew the Church and satisfy many Christians who are longing for an orthodox expression of catholic faith that celebrates diversity, and a song for the world that resonates with the authentic and godly instincts of twenty-first century human beings.

So let us not worry about what the rest of the Church may say. Rather let us be true to the revelation of the love of God that we have been given.

My definition of mission is see what God is doing in the world, then roll up your sleeves and join in! We have got to stop starting with the Church and play catch up with God. Let us catch up with the Holy Spirit who is already showing us in the world the many different ways there are to be human.

But the proclamation of this radical good news for the world will bring us conflict. In today's Gospel reading Jesus tells his followers, 'If any want to become my followers, let them deny themselves and take up their cross and follow me' (Mark 8:34). This does not mean simply wearing a cross or fixing a fish symbol to the back of your car. What Jesus means is where and how will you be crucified because of your witness to me? Where will the goodness and the newness of the Gospel – the sacrificial loving and the penetrating vision of the kingdom – bring you into conflict and strip you down?

> For those who want to save their life will lose it,
> and those who lose their life for my sake,
> and for the sake of the gospel, will save it.
> For what will it profit them to gain the whole world
> and forfeit their life? (Mark 8:35-6)

We have to face the cost of being faithful to the Gospel. We also have to be clear that if we do not become a movement with good news for the world then we do not deserve to prosper and we will soon fade away.

The words 'mass' and 'mission' have the same root. They are to do with being sent. The Eucharist is not the hot bath and the end of the day, where we lie back and forget all our troubles, it is more like the cold shower at the beginning of the day to zap us up and energise us for what lies ahead. Sunday is not the last day of the week, but the first – the new Sabbath, or even as some spiritual writers have called it, the eighth day – the new creation.

May the extended Eucharist which we have experienced together energise us for mission. We have got it. Now we need to flaunt it!

O sing a new song to the Lord.

Appendix:
A Living Catholic Tradition*

Averil Cameron

I imagine that in inviting me to address the fourth of Affirming Catholicism's five 'Guidelines for Christian Living Today', entitled: 'We work for a living catholic tradition to carry the gifts of the past into the future', it was thought that, as a historian, I would have something to say on the past. In fact to a historian sensitive to the interpretation of texts almost every word in the guideline is dynamite. Let me start with 'the gifts of the past'. *Which* past, or which parts of the past, and *whose* past? L. P. Hartley's novel, *The Go-Between*, opens with the words 'The past is a foreign country. They do things differently there.'

But the foreignness of the past is only one of its problems. Even more serious is the fact that as David Lowenthal pointed out in his very interesting book, *The Past is a Foreign Country*,[1] our sense of the past is constructed by ourselves: nobody can know the whole picture; so we do the only thing we can, which is to select the bits that we want to emphasise, and even then the content of what is selected is not given, so much as tailored to fit our own agendas. History is about social memory.[2] It supplies the collective past which we need at any given time. But real history isn't nearly so straightforward. If you doubt this, try a little historical criticism – or try asking several different people you know how they remember the same event. Don't forget,[3] there is not one gospel in the canonical New Testament, but *four*, and they tell different stories.

So the seemingly innocent phrase 'the gifts of the past'

*© Averil Cameron 1998

conceals a high degree of selection – *which* gifts, and *which* past? In this dilemma, to say, as people often do, that Christianity is a historical religion, solves nothing, because while it sounds so obvious and so persuasive, it actually begs the same questions.

So much by way of introduction. After the Lambeth Conference, I was tempted to tear this up and start again with a paper on the proper use of Scripture. However, I thought I had better stick to the guidelines, and so I would like to start by considering the meaning of 'tradition'. As a historian, I am predisposed to respect tradition. Our founders here thought that they were restoring the forgotten tradition of the Fathers and the Early Church, and as Warden of Keble, speaking in Keble College Chapel, I can hardly get away from tradition. But what kind of tradition do we mean? The guideline refers to a 'living tradition', that is, to an ongoing collective sense, and not only to the legacy of the past. But as Rowan Williams has put it so well,[3] the Church comprises a 'network of accountability to the past and the present'. 'Tradition' in its historical sense crops up so often (and has done in the past) that we have to start from there; I will call it tradition type A. I want to argue that *all* tradition, including the tradition of the past, is living tradition.

Tradition

So, despite its derivation from the Latin *tradere* – to hand down – even tradition type A is living; it cannot be regarded as an essence, something undisputed and handed down intact by 'the undivided Church' and 'the Fathers'. In any case these two terms are too vague to be useful. If they fulfil a purpose, it's an emotive one. What *is* this tradition to which everyone appeals? Even in historical terms, we know surprisingly little about Christians in the first two centuries, and what we know is geographically extremely patchy. In Alexandria, Carthage, Edessa – all of them to become great centres of Christian tradition – the Church only becomes visible to us in our historical sources at the turn of the second and third centuries. The Roman Church itself was Greek-speaking into the third century, and so hardly 'Roman' at all. As for Christian theology and the primacy of Scripture, when Christian teaching was in the process of being formed, the New Testament canon was still not finally settled, and knowledge of the Old Testament among gentile Christians was still remarkably limited. Christian self-definition was still fluid enough for there to be competing ideas of what it should be, and Christians and Jews were as yet far from clearly separated.[4] We tend to forget how much time and effort the early Christians spent in trying to differentiate themselves from Jewish tradition. Our fundamentalist friends have probably forgotten, for example, that there were influential voices within the Church which did not consider that the biblical books of Mosaic law, especially Deuteronomy and Leviticus, on which some of them so much rely, should be included in the Christian canon at all.[5] Moses brought the Law, but Israel rejected it, and in consequence the 'second law' (Deuteronomy) was laid upon the Jews as a punishment. It followed that Christians were freed from it. Food for thought there.

But in their search for catholic revival, Keble's founders and their friends in the Oxford Movement didn't focus on Scripture so much as on tradition. They enthusiastically delved into the writings of the Early Fathers, and brought out their works in new editions and translations. But when they appealed to apostolic and patristic tradition they too looked back more with idealised nostalgia than critical discernment – not surprising, perhaps, in an age when the very idea of biblical criticism was still scandalous in itself. I am glad to remember that Edward Talbot, the first Warden of Keble, contributed to *Lux Mundi* which caused a sensation for its questioning of Scripture;[6] but there was still a long way to go in approaching the Fathers critically.

Tradition is a wonderful and comforting and necessary thing. But we can't take it for granted, and we shouldn't confuse it with nostalgia for the good old days of the past. I will take one or two examples drawn from my own work of how that supposedly sacrosanct 'tradition' was actually formed. They will show that living tradition was as much then as now something to be sought and fought for, with pain and trouble. It is not just a given.

My first example is from the Council of Nicaea in 325, from which came the basis of the Nicene Creed. So fundamental has the Nicene Creed been taken to be that the western insertion of the one Latin term *filioque* was enough in the end to cause the eastern and western Churches to split. Yet the circumstances of that Creed's production, and of the Council which produced it, are hardly inspiring.

Citing Wilfred Knox, Geoffrey Rowell wrote in *The Vision Glorious* that with the ending of persecution, the Church 'was able to articulate her teaching and put into a coherent form the sense in which she interpreted in the light of Christian experience *the original deposit of faith which she had received from her Lord.*'[7] This is pretty disingenuous. Edward Norman, in an interesting article about ecclesiology and authority taken from a lecture delivered at Lambeth 1998 and reprinted recently in the *Church Times*,[8] starts from a similar position, but at least he sees that the concept of a 'deposit of faith' is a slippery one. The truth at Nicaea was rather that Constantine knocked the heads of the bishops together in his anger and dismay at finding that Christians were quarrelling with each other over what he thought were trivialities. In reality the Council was far from ecumenical: there were hardly any western bishops present, and the traditional number of participants (318) came into the tradition only because it was the number of the biblical servants of Abraham. Whether Constantine supplied the key word 'consubstantial' from the prompting of the Holy Spirit or from his friend the bishop of Cordoba we can hardly tell. The bishops at Nicaea were neither the first nor the last to be seduced by a strong-minded monarch, and many who signed had gone along promising themselves that they wouldn't do it.

According to Eusebius, the scene at the dinner party given by Constantine for the bishops after the ending of the Council was like Christ among his apostles in heaven – except for the soldiers with drawn swords who guarded the imperial palace.

It is a curious – but in these circumstances perhaps not surprising – feature of the Council of Nicaea that many of the main participants including the emperor changed their position within a few years, and that for more than a

130

generation it remained on the books while the prevailing opinion in many quarters deviated from it.

There is no contemporary official record of the Council. We know about it chiefly from two contemporaries, Bishop Eusebius of Caesarea, and the future saint Athanasius, who attended as a deacon. They were men poles apart, and their accounts are as different as can be imagined. Eusebius went to the Council under a cloud, having been denounced by a synod held only months before at Antioch. But he enthusiastically joined the emperor's side, and wrote about the Council's decisions in glowing but conveniently unspecific terms – for he too was later to oppose the Nicene position again, and to rejoice when Athanasius was exiled for supporting it.

The tactics of Athanasius, to put it frankly, were not much better, though admittedly (unlike Eusebius) he did not change his theological position. He was a fighter, and in a series of tendentious works written to justify himself during the course of his several exiles through the influence of the enemies of Nicaea, he gives a partial and very one-sided account of what happened. How then to choose between bland omission and tendentious claims? Yet this is the Athanasius so admired by Newman, and the author of one of the greatest works on the Incarnation. The same man has been described by a recent scholar, not without justification, as a 'thug'.

Article XXI of the Thirty-Nine Articles admits that councils may err. My question is not whether the conclusions of Nicaea were right, but how we can know what really happened and whether this is the mind of the Church in action. A blind attachment to tradition or to 'authority' won't help.

The men of the Early Church were, I fear, people like us, or some of us at least, for of course as far as councils were concerned, they were all men. Just to underline the point, I quote from the opening of a recent article (written by a woman): 'The Fathers are the authoritative teachers of the Christian Church in the centuries of its formation within Graeco-Roman culture. Patristics, the study of their writings, conveys almost overwhelmingly the weight of male authority.'[9] Men though they were, they failed, and succeeded, as we do, and their motives were not always pure, even if they were brilliant theologians. They fought to form and control the tradition of their day as we do ours.

My second example comes a bit nearer the bone, even though it does not involve the creeds. One of the greatest of the eastern Fathers was John of Damascus. Among his voluminous works is one called *The Fount of Orthodoxy*, and he was much taken up with combating the heresies of his day and arguing against earlier ones. It is well known that the Oxford Movement and their followers were much drawn to the eastern Church. One should ask why this was. It represented for them the purer tradition of the first councils without later Roman accretions. For the eastern Church, it was and is an article of belief that everything was contained in Scripture and the Fathers – with an emphasis on the latter; nothing else was justified or necessary. But even here a little tweaking takes place; and the last two of the seven ecumenical councils – those of Constantinople in 681 and Nicaea in 787 – tell a rather different story. It was argued by John of Damascus himself that there was also an *unwritten* tradition, complementary to and *coexisting* with the words of the Scriptures and the Fathers. John appealed to tradition as a basic principle of argument, but tradition for him was something much broader than what it officially consisted of.

There is more to tell in this particular story. So great was the respect for tradition in theological argument that, like others before him, John's argumentation operated by piling up proof texts from earlier Fathers. There were collections of such quotations that a writer could draw on, and emend or expand. But it all got out of hand. In the council of 681 (the Sixth Council), so many dubious quotations were produced that rules of evidence were laid down: no fragments or extracts would be accepted, only whole books, and even they had to be verified from copies in the Patriarchal Library at Constantinople. The extant records of the Seventh Council in 787 largely consist of discussions of such proof texts. The most powerful evidence that could be cited was universally recognised to consist of extracts from writings of earlier Fathers – in other words, tradition. The argument was about the authenticity of the tradition cited, but not about the issue of tradition itself. But what precisely belonged in the tradition was another matter, and bishops were not above fabricating evidence to support their case.

Another vital question is how individual councils – the embodiment of tradition – have come to be recognised as authoritative. The Seventh Council, which was also the second Council of Nicaea and which vindicated the use of religious images, is regarded as ecumenical. But it was by no means the only council in the period, nor did it have the final say. There were councils before and after it, just as there were numerous other synods and councils before and after the first Council of Nicaea in the fourth century. So what does it take to make a council ecumenical? Not sheer numbers or representation, as we saw from the case of Nicaea. By those standards the Lambeth Conference qualified far better, but, as we saw, it does not rank as a council, even for Anglicans, only as a 'conference'. In fact in passing resolutions, you could say that it betrayed its own ambiguous status. Those who agree will certainly want to portray its resolutions as normative, while those who disagree will want to say that they are not binding. To take another early example, the Fifth Council, held in Constantinople in 553–4, was as biased towards the easterners as Nicaea. Moreover, it found itself in a real dilemma when the bishop of Rome stayed away, even though he was present in Constantinople at the time. This made things very difficult, because a full complement of five patriarchs throughout was thought essential for the status of the Council. The deacon of St Sophia who later wrote about its proceedings dealt with the problem of his non-attendance by simply pretending he was there.

Again, 'tradition' was being formed – should we say manufactured? Contrary to what you might think, I haven't given these examples just so as to dwell on the seamy side, but rather to show again that the experiences, and perhaps even the tactics, of these earlier generations were no different from our own. If the Holy Spirit was working through them, he may have felt sometimes that they were not always very helpful.

So tradition has always been living. At no time was it

finished and complete. It was always being made, out of many different possibilities, no doubt with much prayer, but also at times with personal anguish, broken friendships, personal betrayals, the heart-searching and emotion so apparent in the letters and documents from the Oxford Movement and more recently in the hearts of the bishops at Lambeth.

Tradition is not the same as 'heritage', either. I can perhaps draw a parallel here from my experience as a member of the Cathedrals Fabric Commission. We are obliged according to the 1990 Measure to give first thought to the preservation of the ancient fabric of cathedrals. Hence we work, quite properly, with English Heritage and for instance the Heritage Lottery Fund. But unlike these two bodies, we in the Commission also have another duty laid down in the Measure, which is to 'have regard' to the function of cathedrals as the seat of the bishop and the centre of worship and mission. The ancient fabric is not to be preserved at *any* cost; if a good enough case can be made, it can be altered for the worshipping needs of the cathedral. But one does not approach such decisions lightly, and the sting and the problem lie in that phrase 'have regard'. We are not instructed as to when exactly to apply it, or how; we are given the decision to make ourselves. Is not this the case with 'tradition' only here the 'object' is not concrete or visible, like the fabric of a great cathedral. It was and is 'living', open to challenge, to some degree fluid.

Catholic

The term 'catholic' in the guideline is hardly less difficult. In the benign sense – what we might call 'catholic' type A – it means 'universal', the whole Church as opposed to a sect, what has always been accepted. The word was used early, but it is a word which makes a claim, and I suspect that it was always tendentious. It is probably of importance that the first person to use it was Ignatius of Antioch, who was also the first to use the term 'Christianity' (*christianismos*), and who was as we know very insistent on episcopal authority. In other words he had an agenda which had to do with defining Christians as a group. At

134

best the term 'catholic' meant 'us', our group, people who agree with us; at worst its meaning slid into 'catholic' type B, where it is used as a word of exclusion, to mark off diversity as heresy.

The members of the Oxford Movement were romantics; they wanted to bring back an idealised lost world of early catholic Christianity contained in the – undifferentiated – works of 'the Fathers'. But the Early Church was not like that. Richard Holloway has written in the *Guardian* that the Early Church was probably like Dr Paisley. I am sure he will not mind if I quote him:

> Tolerance is something Christianity learned from secular history rather than from its own unaided efforts. Christians have thought of *in*tolerance as a virtue, and that it was right to per-secute those who disagreed with us in order to save their immortal souls.[10]

This was certainly true of the so-called catholic and undivided Church idealised by the Oxford Movement. Take Constantine's mode of address to heretics, in an official decree:

> You opponents of truth, enemies of life and counsellors of ruin! Everything about you is contrary to the truth, in harmony with ugly deeds of evil; it serves grotesque charades in which you argue falsehoods, distress the unoffending, deny light to believers. (VC III.64.2)

There is much more in the same vein. Having settled matters, as he thought, at the Council of Nicaea, the emperor did not hesitate to close down heretic places of worship, destroy their books and try to bring them into the catholic Church: thus, Eusebius disingenuously claims in about AD 338,

> The parts of the common body were united together and joined in a single harmony, and alone the catholic Church of God shone forth gathered unto itself, with no heretical or schismatic group left anywhere in the world. (III.66.3)

I have just finished writing about Eusebius' account of these vital years, and believe me, absolutely none of his statements can be taken for granted, and certainly not this one.

Newman was led along the path to Rome by accepting at face value a similarly facile definition of the catholic Church as presented at the Council of Chalcedon in 451 – a political shenanigans if ever there was one. He also admired the bishop of Rome at the time of Chalcedon for what he thought was a splendid example of papal authority. Instead of exposing the records to critical suspicion, he accepted the terms given, applied his own logic and came to identify the Church of England with the Monophysites condemned by Chalcedon and the Donatists opposed by Augustine, in other words with heretics and schismatics. But the texts themselves, which are the only way through which we can access the 'tradition', do not support this monolithic view, and never did. In these matters there never *was,* in those famous phrases, 'the judgement of the whole world' or 'that which is believed by all and always has been'.

My model of the Church's history both in the early days and now is not one of certainty but of search, indeed, of struggle and competition. The Scriptures manifestly did not drop fully formed out of heaven, and even if we leave out all the later centuries and go back as the Oxford Movement did to the Early Church in the quest for purity, the 'tradition' was not constant, and was formed only by toil and strife. As a historian I tend to subscribe to the not very fashionable view that the *people* of history were just like us. They tried and struggled to find the right way forward just as we do. They did not have all the answers.

We also have the right and duty to make that tradition a live one. My model of a living catholic tradition is of one that preserves the best but does not forbid the exercise of reason. If I thought otherwise I could not subscribe to it myself. I could not be a fundamentalist if I tried, and I certainly don't want to be.

Let me say a few words about what it meant to come to Keble College as Warden. I did not seek it out, and I was perhaps not particularly well prepared for what it would mean. The weight of tradition hangs very heavy not only on Keble's foundation and its past Christian history, but on

Oxford generally, and on the colleges in particular. It is a male tradition too. The atmosphere of the Oriel common room in the 1820s and 1830s is not dead! A large number of the older members of Keble are still in orders, and many of them are sensitive to any dilution of College tradition, and say so in no uncertain terms. But a good number from this generation also wrote to me when I was elected to express their warm support – 'about time too', they said. Different again are very many of the students, who simply see Keble as a large and popular college where (I fear) they think they will have a good time. They are blissfully unaware that Keble was ever controversial, or that its architecture was ever ridiculed ('It isn't a college, it's a Fair-Isle sweater!' – Oscar Wilde said that everything about Oxford was glorious – except Keble); rather refreshingly, they just think it is beautiful.

I believe my role is on the one hand to try to keep a balance but on the other to help to move things on. The old ways – when there was still compulsory chapel and a steady flow of ordinands – have gone. We are a very forward-looking college nowadays. A good many of our Fellows are down-to-earth hard-working academics who are not very bothered by College traditions. But this great building stands for something important and it is our job to try to make sure that that continues. Before I came I was given some advice by Dennis Nineham, who is one of the three previous Wardens of Keble still living in Oxford; it was that as Warden you have to love everybody. As a piece of advice it took my breath away at the time, but I think I am beginning to see what he meant.

I was definitely not elected by the current Fellows because I was interested in the Early Church or because I was thought to be pro-Chapel. It would not surprise me if the opposite was the case. But I did find myself in a role, and I was presented with a choice as to how to carry it out. Now I may be a historian, and therefore drawn to the past, but I read Greats at Oxford, and that has made me a natural sceptic. I have recently even been accused by an old friend of being a cultural relativist. I was also, like Richard Holloway, a child of the sixties. When I was a recent graduate then, we thought we were throwing off tradition and entering a new world of freedom, and a lot of that has stayed with me – especially in my academic work. Since then I have discovered deconstruction and postmodernism. My friend Victor Stock can confirm that I still find it pretty difficult to bring myself to subscribe for example to dogmatic statements like those in the Creed or, as the early Christians would have put it, to 'confess the name'. But I always knew that I was still searching, and when I came here I did not hesitate. It was not because of the tradition. But the tradition helped. That is the good part of tradition. As a historian I already loved the sense of connecting with the past. One of the most attractive features of the Orthodox Church for me is the sense that one has of being surrounded by the Fathers as though there has been no break. You are surrounded in an Orthodox church by familiar pictures of the Fathers, and to an Orthodox monk they are as alive as anyone he knows today. Sitting in the Warden's stall in Keble Chapel is a different experience, but an equally moving one.

I believe Christianity is about continuing to search, and that the strength and persistence of Christianity over two millennia is that it allows – or better, that it *demands* – this search. It requires of us as human beings and individuals continually to aspire, not to regard revelation as finished and complete. The Christian search seems to me to be all about the old philosophical and psychological problem of understanding and balancing the *self* and the *other* – how do they relate to each other, and how must we understand them? Fitting our sense of ourselves into our sense of society, and of the world – what I have called elsewhere a total system, which does not mean a closed system or a set of dogmas laid down nearly two thousand years ago, but a living and growing understanding and a living faith. The Church that I want to see is one that is capable of mediating that necessary sense of community and continuity while also allowing the personal religious conscience and experience. This was why the Lambeth Conference of 1998 – or at least the part that was reported – was such a disappointment. Pusey himself in an optimistic moment claimed that 'the true Catholic system' is truly inclusive, able to embrace apparent opposites without being authoritarian.[10] That is almost too much to imagine. To my mind there is a dire shortage of people in the Church who can give a lead, help others to use their own discernment, and see that Christianity does not have to be about blind faith or following Scripture literally. This above anything ought to be the job for the future for Affirming Catholicism. Not only affirming, but *teaching* how to think as modern or I suppose I should say, postmodern Christians. God has given us human choice, human aspirations and human dignity, and the least we can do in return is to use them properly.

Notes

1 Cambridge, 1985.
2 See James Fentress and Chris Wickham, *Social Memory* (Oxford: Blackwells, 1992).
3 'Does it make sense to speak of pre-Nicene orthodoxy?', in Rowan Williams, ed., *The Making of Orthodoxy. Essays in Honour of Henry Chadwick* (Cambridge, 1989), pp. 1–23, at p. 18.
4 Judith Lieu, *Image and Reality. The Jews in the World of the Christians in the Second Century* (Edinburgh, 1996).
5 On this see M. Simon, *Verus Israel* (Eng. trans, 1996 ed.), pp. 88–91.
6 Charles Gore, ed., *Lux Mundi. A Series of Studies in the Religion of the Incarnation* (London, 1889).
7 Geoffrey Rowell, *The Vision Glorious. Themes and Personalities of the Catholic Revival in Anglicanism* (Oxford, 1983), p. 230.
8 *Church Times*, 6 Aug. 1998, pp. 21–3, at p. 22.
9 Gillian Clark, 'The old Adam: the Fathers and the unmaking of masculinity', in Lin Foxhall and John Salmon, eds., *Thinking Men, Masculinity and its Self-Representation in the Classical Tradition* (London, 1998), pp. 170–82, at p. 170.
10 *Guardian*, 25 July 1998.
11 Preface to his translation of J. Surin, *The Foundations of the Spiritual Life* (1874 ed.), quoted by A. M. Allchin in Geoffrey Rowell, ed., *Tradition Renewed. The Oxford Movement Conference Papers* (London, 1986), p. 235.

Note on Affirming Catholicism

Affirming Catholicism is a movement within the Church of England and the Anglican Communion, formed in 1990. We affirm that the Anglican Communion is holy, catholic, apostolic; that the riches of the catholic tradition are needed throughout the Church to further the Christian mission; and that genuine catholicism means including lay and ordained people in church government, and both men and women in the three-fold ministry. The agenda of Affirming Catholicism has been more fully defined in our Five Guidelines to Christian Living Today. These Guidelines state that our vocation as Christians and as a movement is to build:

1) disciplined lives of regular prayer, study and worship;
2) commitment to the social and moral transformation of the world;
3) models of love and community for all seeking to follow the Gospel;
4) a living catholic tradition to carry the gifts of the past into the future;
5) liturgy to inspire holiness and relate the greatness of God to his people today.

In association with Darton, Longman and Todd, we publish a series of theological booklets on pressing and controversial topics, as well as on aspects of Anglican history and our tradition. We also publish a journal-in-book-format, *Third Millennium*, which aims to promote informed catholic theological thinking about the life and faith of Christians today in the light of tradition. Each issue of *Third Millennium* focuses on a specific topic. The first three titles (price £3 each) are *Sex and the Christian Tradition;*

140

Vision or Revision – Seeing through the Sacraments; and *Ask and Receive – How Liturgy Responds to Life*. Our best-selling publication is *This Is Our Faith* (£4.95), a popular presentation of Anglican Church teaching edited by Canon Dr Jeffrey John and published by the Redemptorists. We also publish *Going for Growth* by Canon Dr Jeffrey John, which is a strategy for mission and good practice to help incumbents of parishes in the central and catholic traditions.

We have 1500 members in the British Isles, the USA, Canada, Australia, New Zealand and Sri Lanka. Locally we are organised in diocesan groups, which maintain mailing lists of local sympathisers in addition to fully paid-up members, and organise programmes of activities. We promote talks, conferences, pilgrimages, study days and quiet days, and help provide educational and other resources for actively committed Anglican associations and individuals. Our next conference at Durham will be in September 2002. At Durham in September 2000 we launched a Millennial Appeal, to raise £500,000 so that we can establish the permanent full-time post of General Secretary, with proper funds to enhance our missionary and educational activities. If you are interested in joining us or supporting us financially, please contact our Secretary, Elizabeth Field, at:

Affirming Catholicism, St Luke's Centre, 90 Central Street, London EC1V 8AQ, UK
Tel: +44 [0]20 7253 1138; Fax: +44 [0]20 7253 1139
or by email: *affcath@affirmingcatholicism.org.uk*
or visit our website at: *www.affirmingcatholicism.org.uk*